Social Studies Made Simple • Grade 6

Social Studies Made Simple

Grade 6

Written by Diane Sylvester

McGraw-Hill
Children's Publishing

A Division of The McGraw-Hill Companies

Published by Frank Schaffer Publications
An imprint of McGraw-Hill Children's Publishing
Copyright © 1997 McGraw-Hill Children's Publishing

Send all inquiries to:
McGraw-Hill Children's Publishing
3195 Wilson Drive NW
Grand Rapids, Michigan 49544

Social Studies Made Simple—grade 6
ISBN: 0-7647-0178-9

Introduction

By the time students reach the sixth grade, they have studied the history of the United States. Ancient history, however, explores new and fascinating information and generates many questions.

Where did the first humans live?

How did humans progress from cave dwellers to modern humans?

How did we learn about early people's lives?

What can we learn from studying early peoples?

Frank Schaffer's Grade 6 *Social Studies Made Simple* leads students through humankind's earliest years. The book provides activities to help students apply what they learn to the time period they are studying and their own lives. Students generally find the study of ancient people and ancient civilizations to be both interesting and entertaining. They are fascinated by the diversity of religions, systems of government, and expressions in art, architecture, music, and drama.

Help students to look at ancient history in light of the experiments that early humans conducted in all forms of social interaction. Pose questions to students that help them to understand that we, too, continue to search for new ideas, new technologies, and new ways to judge the rules of conduct by which we govern our lives.

Students should begin to understand that the study of ancient history helps us all to appreciate the great ingenuity of our ancestors and to recognize—and learn from—their mistakes and their triumphs. During the course of their studies, students will gain practice in chronological thinking, historical comprehension, historical analysis and interpretations, historical research, and historical issue-analysis and decision-making.

FS-23226 Social Studies Made Simple ▪ © Frank Schaffer Publications, Inc.

Social Studies

CONCEPTS

John Kennedy said, "There is an old saying that the course of civilization is a race between catastrophe and education. In a democracy such as ours, we must make sure that education wins the race." The study of ancient history may help your students prepare for that race.

- Historical thinking requires students to evaluate evidence, develop causal analysis skills, to construct sound historical arguments, and develop perspectives that will help them make informed decisions in contemporary life.

- Early man-made contributions to the progress of man in five spheres: social, scientific, economic, political, and cultural.

- By understanding how humans developed in these five spheres, we can appreciate the record of aspirations, strivings, accomplishments, and failures that characterize human development.

- Studying ancient history equips students with the historical perspectives to understand contemporary issues and to contribute meaningfully to the democratic processes.

RESOURCES

General Information on Ancient Civilizations:

Hunter, Erica. *Cultural Atlas for Young People, First Civilizations.* NY: Facts on File, 1994.

Millard, Dr. Anne. *How People Lived.* New York: Dorling Kindersley, 1989.

Oliphant, Margaret. *The Earliest Civilizations.* New York: Facts on File, 1993.

Ancient Egypt, Kush

Hart, George. *Eyewitness—Ancient Egypt.* New York: Knopf, 1990.

Marston, Elsa. *The Ancient Egyptians.* New York: Benchmark Books, 1996.

Putnam, James. *Eyewitness—Pyramid.* New York: Knopf, 1994.

Steedman, Scott. *Pockets, Ancient Egypt.* London: Dorling Kindersley, 1995.

Ancient China

Cotterell, Arthur. *Eyewitness—Ancient China.* New York: Knopf, 1994.

Temple, Robert. *The Genius of China.* New York: Simon & Schuster, Inc., 1986.

Ancient India

McNair, Sylvia. *Enchantment of the World,* India. Chicago: Children's Press, 1991.

Srinivason, Radhika. *India.* New York: Marshall Cavendish, 1990.

Ancient Israel

Dhamir, Hana, Ed. *The Young Readers' Encyclopedia of Jewish History.* New York: Viking Kestrel, 1987.

Ancient Greece

Clure, John, Ed. *Living History: Ancient Greece.* London: Harcourt Brace & Co., 1994.

Pearson, Anne. *Eyewitness Books: Ancient Greece.* New York: Knopf, 1992.

Schomp, Virginia. *Cultures of the Past: The Ancient Greeks.* New York: Benchmark Books, 1996.

Sutcliff, Rosemary. *The Wanderings of Odysseus.* New York: Delacorte Press, 1995.

Wilkinson, Philip. *Mysterious Places: The Mediterranean.* New York: Chelsea House Publishers, 1994.

Ancient Rome

Corbishley, Mike. *What Do We Know About Romans?* New York: Peter Bedrick Books, 1991.

Nardo, Don. *The Roman Empire.* San Diego: Lucent Books, 1994.

Simon, James. *Eyewitness; Ancient Rome.* New York: Knopf, 1990.

The Cro-Magnon People

Time: c. 35,000–27,000 BC

Location: France and Spain

Significance: Cro-Magnon people were more advanced than Neanderthal people and used a variety of tools and domesticated animals and plants. Showing great artistic skill, they painted pictures of animals deep in caves. Cro-Magnons looked like modern people, lived in tribes, and traveled long distances to trade.

FALLING INTO ANCIENT HISTORY

Class Activity

In 1940, four boys were playing in a forest when their dog disappeared down a hole. One of the boys lowered himself into the hole to rescue the dog. To his surprise, he found himself in a cave whose walls were covered with magnificent paintings. Lead a discussion on whether your students would have followed the dog into the hole. Would they have been afraid of anything in particular? Talk about the sights, the smells, and what they might have felt or sensed going down the hole and being in the cave. Have students make lists of all the things—real and imaginary—that they could find in a cave. Write some "cave vocabulary" on the board including words like *stalagmite*, *stalactite*, *grotto*, and *cavern*. Then have students write creative stories about what happened when they discovered a cave. For atmosphere, darken the room.

Art Project

Hand Paintings

Some of the artwork in the Lascaux, France, cave includes handprints. Experts speculate that the prints could be the signature of the artist or a way of stating that the artist was real. Ask your students to think of reasons why a cave painter would add a handprint to his drawing. Supply art paper so students, working alone or with a partner, can make designs of handprints using only those pigments Cro-Magnon artists used for handprints: black, brown, red, or violet. Students can dip their hands, or parts of their hands, into pie tins of paint and then stamp their hands on the paper.

SAVING THE ORIGINAL

Class Activity

After a fungal growth appeared on the Lascaux wall paintings in 1963, the cave was closed to the public. In 1983, an exact replica called Lascaux II opened. Have students do research on funguses. Why would scientists be worried about a fungal growth? Are there any good funguses? Ask your students if they can think of any places in the United States that should be closed to the public because of potential environmental damage. Have students pretend they are writing to a public official to make a recommendation on why a certain monument should be closed and how it can be done successfully. Include plans for the "II" version of the monument.

FS-23226 Social Studies Made Simple ▪ © Frank Schaffer Publications, Inc.

FINDING YOUR WAY

Cro-Magnon people are named for the French site where their remains were first discovered. One important site is Lascaux Cave, located on a site near Montignac in Dordogne, France. Help students find the spot on a map and locate the nearest large city. Determine the distance from Lascaux to Altamira, Spain, which has other Cro-Magnon sites. How far is Altamira from Lascaux? Work with students to plot all Cro-Magnon sites on a map. Use a scale to determine distances.

THE GREAT HALL OF BULLS

The main cavern of Lascaux in France is called the Great Hall of Bulls. The cavern has a frieze over its walls depicting huge polychrome bulls and horses. The largest animal is 19 feet long. Smaller bison, stags, a bear, and mythical spotted and two-horned animals also appear on the walls. Plan a class mural for a cave wall. Include some animals familiar to Cro-Magnon people, a mythical animal or two, and handprints. If it is appropriate, turn off the lights and have students work by flashlights.

DATELINE: ALTAMIRA

In 1879, a nine-year-old Spanish girl, Maria de Sautuola, made an exciting discovery. As Maria's father, an amateur archaeologist, dug inside the entrance to Altamira Cave, Maria wandered inside, entered a dark hole, and saw big red and black animals painted on the ceiling. Have students imagine they are television reporters "on location" for the moment when Maria leaves the cave. What will they ask her? Can they tell the story and still protect the site from sightseers?

TOURING ALTAMIRA

Make your classroom into an Altamira room. Paint on brown butcher paper to simulate cave walls and put paper on the undersides of tables to simulate ceiling paintings. Have students form tour companies to take tourists through their cave and invite younger children.

MAGIC RITUALS

Some archaeologists believe that magic rituals were performed deep in the dark interior of a cave to promote a good hunt, to seek better weather conditions, or to ensure the physical well-being of the tribe. The paintings may have been part of the ritual. Role-play one of the rituals or write a poem describing the events.

Cave Paintings

Complete the following activities.

1. One room in Lascaux cave is called the Shaft of the Dead Man. Here ancient Cro-Magnon artists painted two-horned rhinoceroses, a dead man, a wounded bison, and a bird caught on a spear thrower. Even scientists are not sure what these drawings mean. In the space below, write your interpretation of the meanings of the drawings.

_____

_____

_____

_____

_____

_____

2. Imagine that you are a Cro-Magnon person sitting around a campfire telling about your most recent long and dangerous hunt. On a separate piece of paper, write the story you told. Then draw a picture of the hunt as you would want it depicted on an interior chamber of a cave.

3. The painters at Altamira used brushes that created lines of different widths and textures. Simple brushes were made by chewing the end of a fibrous stick or by shredding feathers and tying them to a coarse quill. On a separate piece of paper, experiment with different tools while you draw a bison. Try your finger, different brushes, a feather, weed, or the fringed end of a twig. Which tool do you like best for the way you want your bison to look? List the various tools you used and put a star by the one you chose for your painting.

4. Artists studying Cro-Magnon art admire the artistic skill and sense of beauty of the paintings. As the renowned art critic, Justmy O. Pinion, write a critique of a painting from Lascaux or Altamira for the art section of a newspaper. Write your critique on the back of this page.

FS-23226 Social Studies Made Simple ■ © Frank Schaffer Publications, Inc.

Çatal Hüyük

Time Period: c. 6500–5000 BC

Location: Anatolia, a large mountainous plateau in south central Turkey

Significance: Çatal Hüyük, one of the earliest known Neolithic towns, developed in the Fertile Crescent. By 6000 BC, the town covered about 32 acres, had about 1,000 houses and about 5,000–6,000 people. Çatal Hüyük's future was limited because the population depended on the obsidian trade and lacked agricultural resources that would enable them to expand.

THE FERTILE CRESCENT
Class Activity

The area of the Middle East where the earliest known civilizations of the ancient world began is called the Fertile Crescent. Wheat, barley, sheep, and goats were plentiful. The soil was light and easy to dig, with enough sunshine and rain for farming. Have students use atlases to locate the boundaries of the Fertile Crescent and the modern countries now located there. Students can work in small groups to find 10 interesting facts about each of the present-day countries. Students can present their findings to the class.

DOORS AND LADDERS
Class Activity

The people of Çatal Hüyük entered their homes through doors in the roofs. The town had no streets or alleyways because people walked along rooftops to get to their houses. The hole, or door, in the roof also allowed smoke to escape. Assign your students the task of remodeling their homes (or their school) in the style of Çatal Hüyük. Encourage them to present creative designs to get to the roofs, to provide security, and to present a pleasing appearance. On the back of the drawing, have students list advantages and disadvantages of a roof entry.

TERRACED ARCHAEOLOGY
Class Activity

Archaeologists at Çatal Hüyük discovered twelve levels of ruins, each from a different time during the 800 years the site was inhabited. As each city was destroyed, the next was built on top of the rubble. Have students make a cross-section of an imaginary 1,000-year-old archaeological site with five levels of ruins and label each time period. In each level, students should draw and label two artifacts that represent the time period. Remind students that the first level is the oldest and the top level the most recent.

TRAVELING FAR
Class Activity

Obsidian from Çatal Hüyük was found 620 miles away at Jericho, and turquoise and copper from the Sinai Peninsula were found at Çatal Hüyük. Locate these places on a map. Ask students to name the modern countries that a trader would travel through going from Çatal Hüyük to the Sinai Peninsula. Then ask them to list items in their own homes that come from other countries and indicate where the items were made. Talk about trade agreements between the United States and other countries. The reproducible page 6, "Trade," focuses on the importance of trade between Çatal Hüyük and other areas.

Religion at Çatal Hüyük

Çatal Hüyük's forty shrines show how important religion was to the people of the town. People entered the shrines through the doors in the roofs, and darkness added to the mystery. Decorated with small clay or stone statues of bulls and rams, the shrines frequently contained real skulls and horns from these animals. Paintings or reliefs showing bulls' heads, human figures, and animals adorned the plaster walls. One interesting mural contains stags; boars; bulls; a volcano; men clad in skins with bows, arrows, clubs, and axes; and various geometric elements.

The bones of the dead were buried beneath plaster platforms which may have been used as altars. Excavations suggest that the bodies of the dead were first left on the rooftops for vultures to pick the bones. Then the skull was removed before the skeleton was wrapped up, put in a basket, and buried.

Complete the following activities:

One wall painting shows priestesses, dressed as vultures, conducting rituals. Another painting shows bulls, leopards, and people; birds are attacking a headless body. Tell your version of the meanings of these ritual components:

priestesses dressed as vultures: _____

_____

_____

birds attacking a headless body: _____

_____

_____

bulls and leopards: _____

_____

_____

On a separate piece of paper, create an imaginary god that combines the forms of a vulture, a leopard, and two other animals. Write a short description of the god; then write a dramatic story about the origin of the god and its powers.

Trade

Archaeologists have found large numbers of obsidian tools in Çatal Hüyük. Obsidian, a dark volcanic glass, is an excellent material for making arrowheads, knives, and other sharp tools and weapons. Obsidians from different volcanoes have different chemical compositions so archaeologists can analyze the obsidian used in the tools to help determine where the obsidian originated, and where it ended up.

Complete the following activities.

1. Based on the information above, explain how scientists may have concluded that Çatal Hüyük was one of the main hubs in obsidian trade between western Anatolia (Turkey), Cyprus, and the areas now in modern Israel, Lebanon, and Syria.

_____

_____

_____

2. High-quality obsidian items were highly valued for trade. Finely polished obsidian mirrors from Çatal Hüyük had no scratches. A ceremonial obsidian dagger with a bone handle shaped like a snake was excavated from a grave site inside a shrine. Design an obsidian tool, piece of jewelry, or luxury item that incorporates some religious symbolism of Çatal Hüyük. Add a short description to your drawing.

3. At the time Çatal Hüyük flourished, money had not been invented so people bartered. Think of something of the same value or importance that you would exchange for each of items below:

Laptop Computer _____   Leather Jacket _____

Soccer Ball _____   Camera with Telephoto Lens

Skateboard _____

Make a list of other things that could have been "traded" when people of different regions met. (Hint: Think of things like language and religion.)

FS-23226 Social Studies Made Simple ▪ © Frank Schaffer Publications, Inc.

Mesopotamia

Time: 5300 BC–539 BC

Location: between the Tigris and Euphrates Rivers

Significance: *Mesopotamia* means "between two rivers." Residents of this fertile plain invented the wheel and writing. From about 5500 BC, farming villages grew up in Sumer in Mesopotamia's southern region, and people gradually coordinated and organized their beliefs, trade, and government. Great city-states like Ur, Eridu, Lagash, Kish, and Babylon developed, each with its own ruler who controlled the land around the city-state. By 2100 BC, Ur had become Mesopotamia's most important city-state.

A SURPLUS MEANS NEW JOBS

Class Activity

Large scale irrigation projects in Mesopotamia resulted in a surplus of grain. Once freed from full-time farming, people were able to develop new skills. New tools for measuring, surveying, and calculating slopes and flow patterns of the canals were invented. Occupations such as artisans, traders, priests, scribes, and merchants developed. A system of government and organized religion arose. Tell students to make a list of the specializations that they think may have emerged in Sumer. What specific jobs would be available in the fields of arts, religion, government, or trade? Discuss with your class which jobs they would have liked and why.

KEEPING TRACK OF TRADE

Class Activity

Wheat, barley, dates, wool, dairy products, and crafts were some of the items Sumerians traded for tools, lumber, stone, and hoes. To keep track of what, and how much, was traded, the Sumerians used clay or stone tokens. Different-shaped tokens stood for different goods and amounts. Traders dropped the tokens into a round clay container and sealed it while the clay was still wet so that no one could change or remove the containers' contents. Eventually, people began to press marks into the wet clay to take the place of the tokens.

Organize a design contest to see who can devise a more practical and useful way to keep track of trade. Students must use clay since that material was available in Sumer. Set a time limit, perhaps 20 minutes. First, students should decide on the system. Then they should think about the tokens, marks, or other symbols and the products they represent. Allow time for each system to be presented to the class. Have the class choose the system that makes record keeping the easiest.

TEMPLES AND ZIGGURATS ···················· Class Activity ······

Temples and ziggurats were the most prominent structures in Mesopotamian communities. Often built on the ruins of previous temples, new temples were usually built on platforms to raise them above their surroundings. As communities grew and prospered, the temple building also expanded. By about 2000 BC, some communities developed huge temple towers, called ziggurats. The ziggurat at Uruk was rebuilt, enlarged, and used continuously for nearly 4,000 years. Both the temple and the ziggurat were made of sun-baked mud bricks and faced with fired bricks that were glazed in various colors. Niches, buttresses, murals, and mosaics adorned the facades of the structures.

Have students form architectural design groups. They need to consult a variety of reference books and then present a plan for constructing a ziggurat. The final product can be an architectural drawing or a model made from miniature sun-dried bricks or sugar cubes. Dedicate the ziggurat to a god. (For example, the ziggurat at Ur was dedicated to the moon god.) Students should make a list of hypothetical people who will be helping them build the ziggurat such as craftsmen, laborers, scribes, and so on.

SUMERIAN CITY STATES ···················· Class Activity ······

Explain to students that Sumer city-states ruled the land and people surrounding a city and collected taxes from them. Each city-state had a royal palace, a ziggurat, an administrative center, houses, and farmers' fields and marshlands. The Sumerians farmed one part of their land for the gods, growing food that was stored and used in times of famine or was traded for goods from abroad. The second part produced food for the priests and temple staff. Citizens farmed the third part to grow food for themselves.

Discuss with the class the responsibilities of their city or town and their state. How different is this from living in a city-state?

ROUND AND ROUND ···················· Class Activity ······

Wheels were probably first invented for pottery making. The first evidence for the use of wheels for transportation comes from Sumer where archaeologists found a clay tablet containing a pictograph of a wheeled cart from about 3200-3100 BC. Knowledge of how these early wheels were constructed comes from "chariot burials" found in the city-states of Kish and Ur. The royal tombs contained vase paintings, scale models, and actual physical remains of chariots, war chariots, and hearse chariots. Vehicles were pulled by domesticated animals, such as oxen, onagers, and the Asiatic ass. Although no conclusive evidence exists, many experts believe that the wheel was invented only once and then diffused to the rest of the world. Challenge students to come up with at least twenty ways to use a wheel. Tell them to imagine they are owners of the Sumer Wheel Company and that they need to be constantly on the lookout for creative uses for the wheel. Have them design a new type of chariot; a new agricultural implement using a wheel; or an unusual toy or game using a wheel.

The Beginning of Agriculture

Before the rise of Sumer, people hunted animals and gathered whatever food they could find in the wild. Slowly, people discovered that certain plants could be cultivated, and they began to rely on the steady supply of food from crops. Fertile areas became more attractive. When the Sumerians developed irrigated agriculture, they no longer needed to rely only on rain to water their crops. Barley and wheat and vegetables grew easily, especially in the rich lands between two rivers that deposited layers of silt during spring floods.

Over hundreds of years, the Sumerians tried different ways to irrigate. At first they carried vessels of water from the rivers to their fields. Later, farmers made narrow breaks in the natural levees along the riverbanks to divert some of the river water onto the fields. Farmers also created small mud dams and collected water in basins. The shaduf, a bailing bucket mounted on a long counterweighted pole, brought water from the dam to the fields. In time, gangs of workers excavated long canals to channel water to fields several miles from the rivers.

Complete the following activities:

1. List in chronological order, the ways farmers used to irrigate their fields.

   a. _____

   b. _____

   c. _____

   d. _____

   e. _____

2. On a separate piece of paper, write a story about an imaginary Sumerian farmer who traveled forward in time to learn about irrigation methods in the desert regions of the United States. Include in your story the things that surprise him the most, the questions he asks his American host, and the suggestions he offers to the modern farmer.

3. The construction of canals required cooperation from the entire community. The people were forced to band together to help each other. Organization, interaction, and innovation were very important. Make a list of rules and regulations on construction and maintenance that you think would have been important to ensure that canal projects ran smoothly in Sumer.

Cuneiform

As the Sumerians' wealth grew, they needed a way to keep accounts. To keep records, they drew little pictures of sheaves of barley or oxen with a reed pen on clay tablets. At first, the pictures, or pictograms, were drawn underneath each other on the wet clay, which was dried in the sun or baked in a kiln to make it hard. Gradually, over about 200 years, these "pictograms" looked less and less like the objects they represented. Instead, they looked like wedges created by the triangular shape of the reed pen. The Sumerians had developed the first form of writing that we know about.

This writing is called *cuneiform,* which means "wedge-shaped." Each pattern stood for a sound or syllable. By adapting the signs and using them together, other words could be formed. About 600 symbols, from a single wedge to complex patterns of 30 wedges, made the daily business of buying and selling in the markets much easier. If a dispute arose, the written contract was checked.

Cuneiform Chart

CUNEIFORM SIGN c. 700 BC	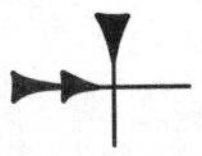				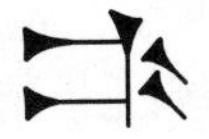		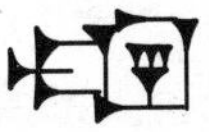		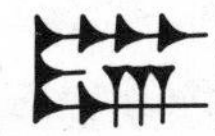
MEANING	god, sky	day, sun	water, seed, son	barley	ox	food, bread	to eat	to walk, to stand	man

Complete the following activities.

1. Using the chart above, practice writing cuneiform. Write a secret message to a friend using cuneiform.

2. Make a wedge-shaped writing tool from an eraser, piece of Styrofoam, or potato. Practice making cuneiform letters by pressing the tool into wet clay or by dipping the tool into ink or paint and stamping it on a piece of paper.

3. Olympic and international signs use pictures to convey a message. Make up a series of signs for your school to aid international visitors. Remember that to be effective, the signs must be simple and their meanings must be clear to someone unfamiliar with the local area and your school.

The Tale of Gilgamesh

The story of Gilgamesh, a king who wanted to be immortal, was part of an oral tradition for hundreds of years before it was finally written down on 12 cuneiform tablets in about 2000 BC. The 3,500-line poem about Gilgamesh was probably the world's first epic, or long poem, and it is probably the best of the literary works of Sumer. The poem was known in at least four languages, and its influence on art and thought spread to many lands and cultures.

Scholars think that the real Gilgamesh was the king of the Sumerian city of Uruk around 2700 BC, but the epic about him is myth, not history, because no historical evidence exists for his exploits. The story does show how the Sumerians viewed their kings and their gods.

The first tablet explains that Gilgamesh is part divine and part human, a great builder and warrior, and the knower of all things on land and sea. When Gilgamesh's pride angered the gods, they made a half-beast, half-man called Enkidu to destroy him. Gilgamesh won the battle that followed, the two became friends, and they helped each other on various adventures. In one adventure, Gilgamesh, who had returned to Uruk, rejected marriage to Ishtar, goddess of love. She sent a divine bull to kill him, but with Enkidu's help the bull is killed.

Tablet VIII tells about the death and funeral of Enkidu and Gilgamesh's journey in search of Utnapishtim, a survivor of the Great Flood, in order to learn the secret of immortality. Utnapishtim explained that he received the secret of life from the unique circumstances of the flood, but he cannot give it to Gilgamesh. He consoled Gilgamesh with news about a secret plant of life which lived at the bottom of the sea. Gilgamesh dived and picked it, but on his way home, while he was taking a nap, the plant was eaten by a snake. Gilgamesh finally returns home, reluctantly accepting death as inevitable.

Pretend that you were one of the scribes responsible for recording the epic of Gilgamesh. You don't like the way the story ends with the snake eating the plant of life. Make changes in this part of the story and then add more adventures for Gilgamesh to accomplish before he can find peace. Illustrate your story with drawings.

FS-23226 Social Studies Made Simple ▪ © Frank Schaffer Publications, Inc.

Spotlight on Babylon

Babylon is an ancient city in Mesopotamia located about 190 miles northwest of Ur and 55 miles south of modern Baghdad, Iraq. Babylon's rise to power began during the 1800s BC about the time when Ur's wealth and importance were declining. King Sumuabum (1894–1881 BC) declared Babylon's independence from Ur and set up a dynasty which lasted almost 300 years.

The sixth ruler of Babylon, and best known, was Hammurabi the Great, who came to power in 1792 BC. Under him, Babylon conquered all of Sumer and Akkad. Hammurabi brought prosperity and peace to Babylon and increased trade with Persia. Except for language, Hammurabi borrowed virtually everything from the conquered Sumer, including writing, art, literature, education, and with a change or two, even religion.

Another well-known ruler of Babylon was Nebuchadnezzar II (605–562 BC). A warlike king, he fortified the city and conducted major military campaigns, including one against Egypt. He also captured Jerusalem, destroyed much of the city, and exiled thousands of Hebrews to Babylon, where they were treated as slaves. Babylon was finally conquered by Alexander the Great in 331 BC.

Map of the City of Babylon

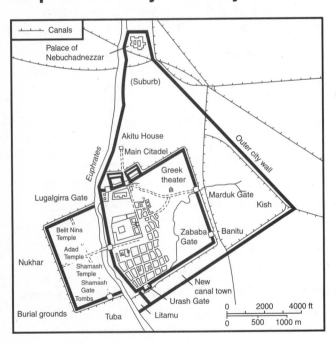

Much of the information about Babylon also came from Herodotus, a fifth century Greek historian who traveled to Babylon and wrote about his impressions. He wrote that Babylon was built in a square which measured 14 miles on each side. It was divided by the Euphrates River which flowed between two walls of brick. Where the ends of streets met these walls, there were large bronze gates to give people access to the river. Merchants and traders could sail their ships from the Persian Gulf up the river and into the city.

(continued on page 13)

A Walking Tour of Nebuchadnezzar's Babylon

You are about to take a walking tour of beautiful Babylon, the largest city in the ancient world—covering about 2,500 acres. Most of the buildings on the tour were either built or renovated by Nebuchadnezzar II. He built or improved most of the fortifications that make the city safe. Some of the walls are so thick that a chariot can travel on the top of them.

Your tour starts at Ishtar Gate, one of eight fortified gates leading to the center to town. It is adorned with glazed bricks decorated with bulls and dragons. The bulls represent the chief god, Murduk, and the dragons symbolize the storm god, Adad. Behind us is Akitu House (New Year Temple), a small temple outside the city. On both sides of Ishtar Gate are fortresses. We will proceed along the Processional Way, its walls decorated with enameled lions. Look to the right and you will see the majestic Hanging Gardens of Babylon.

After we pass the Holy Gate, the Processional Way angles right and we have a good view of the great temple of Marduk (Esagilia) and its ziggurat, Etemenanki (also known as the Tower of Babel). At the uppermost level is a 300-foot-tall temple decorated in blue glaze. As we cross over the great Euphrates River on a bridge built on brick piles, notice that the streets are laid out in a grid. Along the Euphrates you will see quays built for trading vessels that sail to many parts of the world. Outside the city walls are the burial grounds. Work your way back to Ishtar Gate, but before you pass through it, look eastward to observe the area of private dwellings with flat roofs and balconies built around central courtyards. Pass through the gate and head northward to Nebuchadnezzar's Palace. This area within the outer city wall has irrigated land.

Try This! For centuries, the Babylonians excelled in astronomy and mathematics. Early astronomers developed calendars based on the phases of the moon. Scientific achievement divided the hour into 60 minutes. Mathematicians introduced place value into mathematics. Choose one of these achievements as the focus of a research project. Include at least one illustration, diagram, or other visual in the project.

Name _____

Hammurabi and Code of Laws

Babylonian ruler Hammurabi (1792 to 1750 BC) wrote one of the most important ancient codes of law. There were 282 laws in all, arranged under headings like family, labor, personal property, real estate, trade, and business. The main principles of the laws were that the strong should not injure the weak and that punishments should fit the crimes.

Hammurabi's laws provided for testimony under oath from witnesses who could be subpoenaed. The laws also gave some legal status to women and protected their property rights. The laws covered all aspects of daily life, such as rates of pay for hiring transportation and rules for trading. Kidnappers, burglars, bandits, and witches were put to death. A man who broke another's leg would have his leg broken as punishment. Crimes punishable by death required a trial before a bench of judges.

According to Hammurabi's Code of Laws, property could be disposed of by sale, lease, barter, gift, dedication, loan, pledge, or bailment. The laws included the doctrine "let the buyer beware." Written marriage contracts, dowry and marriage settlements, and alimony and child support were all provided for. Wives were permitted to divorce for desertion, cruelty, or neglect.

Hammurabi's laws were carved in stone and displayed in all the major cities of his kingdom. Archaeologists found the best preserved examples on a seven-foot high monument of black diorite at Susa, Iran, in 1901. Hammurabi died in 1750 BC. Weak kings followed, and Babylon finally collapsed in 1595 BC.

1. Pretend that you are in charge of law making in your classroom. Make a list of five situations which you think should be covered by law. Then create laws that you think are fair and equitable for your classmates.

_____

_____

_____

2. Define the saying "let the buyer beware." Do you think the idea is a good one? Explain why or why not?

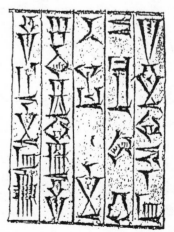

_____

_____

_____

_____

Ancient Egypt

Time: 2686–1069 BC (one of several chronologies used by historians)

Location: along the Nile River from the Delta to Nubia

Significance: one of the earliest civilizations with a centralized government, writing, and irrigation; a great number of monuments survived to aid in learning about Egyptians.

THE SOURCE

Class Activity

Ancient Egypt was mostly desert. The Nile River, which stretches for 600 miles through a long, narrow corridor called the Nile Valley, was the center of Egyptian lives. Take your students on an imaginary trip along the Nile. Use a large map so students can follow your description. First, locate Burundi in central Africa where the Nile originates. Follow the river as it flows through Uganda into Lake Victoria and then into Lake Albert. When it flows through the rocky hills of Sudan, it is known as the White Nile. Then locate the highland region of Ethiopia where the Blue Nile originates. At Khartoum, the two rivers join to form the Nile. Continue your journey to the delta region where the Nile empties into the Mediterranean Sea.

AWAITING THE FLOOD

Class Activity

The Nile River flooded in July, and the floodwaters carried rich soil which was deposited over the fields. The Egyptians called this period the "inundation." After the inundation, farmers planted seeds. Egyptians learned to save enough flood water to last the whole year by cutting canals and ditches to store the water and carry it to the fields. Discuss with your students ways that the environment affected Egyptian history. For example, periodic, long-term decreases in the Nile might have created social stress and political and military conflicts. Increases might have meant more food and a more stable government. Then have students brainstorm ways that the environment may affect the present.

THINK TANKS

Group Activity

Steps taken in modern-day Egypt regulate the flow of the Nile. The Nile Dam, north of Cairo, was built in the first half of the nineteenth century. The Aswan Dam was completed in 1968. These dams freed the farmers from their dependence on the annual flood and made it possible to provide regular irrigation throughout the year. A loss of great quantities of fertile Nile mud blocked by the dams resulted, however. Have students form "think tanks" whose task it will be to find ways the farmers can have the benefits of the dams but retain the availability of the fertile mud. Each think tank should present its findings and suggestions to the class.

MOVING ON WATER

Egypt's highway was the Nile, and boats were the most important form of transportation. Small boats were made from bundles of papyrus stalks lashed together with ropes and propelled by paddles or long poles. Because wood was so scarce, only larger boats, funeral barges, warships, and seagoing ships were built of wood. Ferries were in constant use for crossing the river, and the wealthy had boats for recreation and pleasure. Give each student a piece of paper and tell the students they have five minutes to list all the ways that a person can move on water. Encourage them to write down real, unusual, or creative ways. When the five minutes are up, have them share some of their more unusual ideas. Your class might be interested in starting a large mural. They can begin by drawing in the Nile with a sample of the plant and animal life found along the river. Then they can add a variety of boats that were used on the Nile. As the students learn more about ancient Egypt, they can add to the mural.

TRADING PARTNERS

Surplus foods like lentils and dried fish and items like papyrus and textiles were exported from Egypt in exchange for luxury items. Egyptian traders exchanged their wares for lapis lazuli (Afghanistan); horses (Asia); gold, copper, ebony, and incense (Nubia and Punt); ivory (Africa); turquoise (the Sinai); and fine cedar wood (Lebanon). Cities flourished along the Nile and bustled with foreign ambassadors, visiting royalty, and sailors. Discuss with your class how ideas, religions, philosophies, inventions, and culture could also be "traded."

In the form of a poem, short story, or a drawing, ask students to describe what it would have been like to live in one of these trading towns. Encourage students to include representations of the hustle and bustle and sights and sounds of the town. To review several civilizations, copy this chart on the board and, either on the board or on a separate piece of paper, have students fill in the sections. Afterward, discuss the similarities and differences among the civilizations.

AREA	DATES	EXPORTS	IMPORTS	TRADING PARTNERS
Çatal Hüyük				
Sumer				
Egypt				

MUSIC AND DANCING

By studying their murals, we know that the Egyptians held colorful celebrations with singers, musicians, and dancers. Egyptian music was never written down, but Egyptologists do know that harps, lutes, drums, flutes, tambourines, cymbals, bells, metal rattles called sistra, and clappers like large castanets were played. Festival crowds chanted and clapped and leapt and twirled to the music.

If possible, have students work in small groups. Instruct the groups to "invent" Egyptian music to play at a festival. Give them a time limit—perhaps 20 minutes—and then have a class recital.

CHARTING THE KINGDOMS

Use the chart below as a review of Ancient Egypt's three kingdoms. Allow students to work with a partner to create a page for a picture encyclopedia of Egypt for young people The partners should focus on one kingdom. The page should have pictures of at least one of the buildings, one of the rulers, and short descriptions of important events.

	Dates	2 Famous Buildings	2 Famous Rulers	2 Events
Old Kingdom				
Middle Kingdom				
New Kingdom				

TV TALK SHOW

Tell your class to imagine that a famous late-night talk show host just hired them to guest host the show while the host is on vacation. The special guests for the first night are an Egyptian pharaoh and a former president of the United States. Inform your class that they can choose the pharaoh and the president from any time period. To prepare for the show, students should make a list of the questions they will ask. They should also supply hypothetical answers for three of the questions. Then have the students plan on a few surprises for the show—perhaps a mystery guest from the Old Kingdom or a musical group that plays at the Great Pyramid. Then have students role-play the show.

TIME CAPSULE

As a review of the unit on Ancient Egypt, tell students that they have been put in charge of the pharaoh's Ancient Egyptian Time Capsule. It is their responsibility to choose twenty items that reflect the times and culture, both social and political. Have students make a list of the items they chose and compare the lists with those of other students. If appropriate, have them defend their choices. They should then decide where they will bury the time capsule and when it should be opened.

WHO'S WHO

Who's Who in Ancient Egypt

····• Class Activity •····

Instruct students to do research in order to choose five famous people who should be included in an Ancient Egyptian *Who's Who*. Students should write down the names of all five people and the claim to fame of each one, but should choose one person for a detailed entry. The entry can include a biography, a picture or two, a map, or a tribute by another Egyptian. Include all entries in a class *Who's Who*.

ANKH

····• Class Activity •····

The ankh is the symbol of life. In art, only gods or kings are portrayed with this symbol. Some works show a god or goddess giving life to a pharaoh by touching his mouth with the ankh. Have your students use an ankh, a series of ankhs, or an ankh as part of another pattern in a design that would be appropriate for stationery, wrapping paper, or a greeting card. Then have students figure out which art process will most successfully transfer the design to the actual item. Finally, have students make the items and display them in the Royal Ankh Gift Shoppe.

SPOTLIGHT ON AKHENATEN

····• Class Activity •····

One New Kingdom pharaoh was Amenophis IV. Some historians think Amenophis may have been mentally unstable, but he was a strong and skillful ruler. He was responsible for replacing the old religion with a new one, the first in history based on the worship of one god, Aten, or the sun disk. Amenophis IV forced people to abandon their old gods and closed their temples. He even changed his name to Akhenaten. At Tell el-Amarna, Akhenaten built Aten's cult center and a new royal capital. There he, his queen Nefertiti, and their children became a "holy family," with the king appearing as virtually the god on Earth. After Akhenaten's death, the priests reinstated the old gods and made Thebes the capital once more. Discuss these questions with your students: Who would Akhenaten anger by changing the country's religion? Why? What would you say if you were pharaoh and had to convince your subjects of the worthiness of the new god? Compare the concept of worshipping one god with the practice of worshipping many gods. Which religions today practice the worship of one god? Which do not?

Art Project

Vulture & Cobra

Before the days of unification, the vulture represented Upper Egypt and the cobra represented Lower Egypt. Other symbols of the pharaoh included the crook and flail. Discuss with your class the things that symbolize the president of the United States. Ask the purpose of a symbolic object and identify the images the object brings to mind. Then have students create a unique flag design for Ancient Egypt using the symbols for a pharaoh. The flags can be drawn on paper and displayed around the classroom.

MUMMIFIED ANIMALS

Class Activity

In Egypt, cats were popular pets and sacred to the goddess Bastet. Cats were often mummified and buried in cat-shaped coffins. Near the pyramids at Saqqara are large animal cemeteries where animal mummies were buried in an intricate system of underground galleries and passages. Burial places for animals have been found for ibises, falcons, baboons, dogs, jackals, crocodiles, rams, bulls, cows, and fish. In one ibis gallery, more than 2 million ibis mummies were buried in painted jars. Have students imagine they are animal rights advocates approaching Egyptian priests with their concerns about the animal gods. Students should write or role-play their approach and include the opinions of the priests. Could Egyptians still worship their favorite animals but not sacrifice so many of them?

IMHOTEP, THE FIRST ARCHITECT

Class Activity

Pyramid building was a milestone in the history of architecture. Builders found unusual ways to use stone instead of mud bricks. The Step Pyramid, designed by architect Imhotep, may have been the first structure built according to architectural plans. The Step Pyramid, built for King Zoser, was a series of six levels stacked on top of each other like steps. Zoser's mummy was placed 80 feet underground beneath the pyramid. If possible, invite an architect to discuss the ways pyramids were built. Challenge students to make blueprints or drawings for a pyramid that uses stone in new and unusual ways.

NEWSPAPER REPORTER

Class Activity

Secret entrances, sealed passages, sacrificed builders, false shafts, and extra passages were all used to foil tomb robbers, yet every known pyramid had been looted by 1000 BC. The only intact king's burial chamber ever found belonged to Tutankhamen. Tell students to imagine they are reporters for the *Vulture & Cobra Times*. This is their first big job! The local pyramid had just been robbed, and they were first on the scene. Tell them to interview the architect, witnesses, even the robbers, and then write the newspaper article. Some students may want to accept the offer to be guest editor for the *Vulture & Cobra Times*. They can write an editorial on the design and safety of pyramids or on another topic that concerns them.

CONTROVERSIAL ISSUE

Class Activity

Although archaeologist Howard Carter won great acclaim for discovering and dismantling King Tut's tomb, many people considered it wrong to disturb the ancient resting place. Discuss this controversial issue with your students. Compare King Tut's tomb excavations to the archaeological digs that take place on Native American sites.

Name _____

Ancient Egyptian School of Architecture

Imagine you are an Egyptian architect commissioned to build a home near the Nile. Using only the materials available to the ancient Egyptians, design a home that will provide shelter, offer protection, be efficient, be comfortable, and be environmentally compatible with the desert. Add furniture, art work, and landscaping if you want. Make your final drawing on a separate sheet of paper and label the rooms. Prepare a statement to accompany the drawing which explains where the materials came from and how you provided for the requirements above. To help you in your plans, here is an excerpt from *"The Pharaoh's Architectural Review Journal":*

Important reminder to architects of the Kingdom of Egypt: the harsh desert has a psychological influence on people who live along the Nile. Keep this in mind when planning your dwelling.

Materials

- Mud bricks will be the principle building material for dwellings, city and temple walls, monuments, forts, and storehouses. The wet clay along the Nile is to be used for bricks. Mix it with sand or, if necessary, chopped barley straw. Knead it with water into a thick paste and pour it into wooden brick molds. Leave out in the hot sun to dry.

- The area around the First Cataracts will provide granite and sandstone.

- The desert and the hills to the east will provide limestone, standstone, and some granite. Copper, manganese, turquoise, and some gold are also available. Because of the great demand for these materials, promotion of trade is essential. Encourage the intensification of mining in order to obtain more resources.

Suggestions

- Build houses to stay cool.

- Mud roofs should be poured over a foundation of reeds and grasses.

- Roof terraces are recommended. A wealthy family can have a large villa with lush gardens and fish-stocked pool and a bathroom.

Provide a materials list with your plan. List the building materials common in the region you chose. What are the attributes of each?

A Hollywood Version of Ancient Egypt

You are going to be hired as a costume designer for a Hollywood movie about ancient Egypt. You need to become an expert in ancient Egyptian clothing. First, you have to decide which character in the movie you want to costume. Two characters are a pharaoh and his wife, but you can choose from a cast of thousands! Your costuming must include the complete outfit—jewelry, shoes, hair accessories.

Mini Fact Page on Clothing

Linen:	Linen is made from the fibers of the flax plant. Most Egyptians wore coarse linen, but wealthier people dressed in a lighter, finer version of the fabric. The finest of all linen was semi-transparent and worn by royalty.
Dyes:	The Egyptians knew about dyes, but most linen was left a natural off-white.
Men's Clothing:	Men wore a kilt-like garment consisting of a straight piece of cloth twisted around the body and tied at the waist. Shirts might be worn. During the New Kingdom, kilts became long and full, and woolen cloaks were worn for warmth.
Women's Clothing:	Women wore straight, tight shifts held up by bands over the shoulders. It was not until nearly 1400 BC that artists first showed women dressed in elaborate garments of translucent linen. These dresses were draped rather than cut to fit and were designed with numerous pleats.
Pharaoh:	For important ceremonies, the pharaoh wore a long kilt and an elaborate cloak with many pleats. Men and women wore elaborate necklaces and gold bracelets.
Footwear:	Usually everyone went barefoot, even the rich. But when shoes were worn, they were sandals made from reeds, like papyrus, and leather.
Make-up:	Men and women painted their eyes. Green eye paint came from malachite; black kohl from galena. Red for lips was made from iron oxide. Women placed incense cones on their wigs. These melted slowly, allowing the scent to soak into their hair.
Care of the Body:	Men were usually clean shaven. Often their bodies were shaved, too. Soda was used for bathing. To counteract the drying effect of the soda, the sun, and the dust, men and women rubbed oils into the skin.

Fill out the following information before you begin a costume design.

Title of the movie: _____

Characters: _____

The character you will costume: _____

Make your designs on the back of this page or on a separate piece of paper.

Egyptian Art

The art of ancient Egypt was produced by teams of painters who painted murals of colorful scenes in tombs, temples, and palaces. The scenes depicted hunting expeditions, banquets, religious ceremonies, family and everyday life, and scenes along the Nile River. The art was highly stylized. The figures were usually in formal poses and given perfect features. The human body was shown in profile with the eyes and chest facing forward and the face and legs viewed from the side. Hieroglyphs were added like a caption to the picture.

Sculpture was another important art form. Copper or bronze tools were used to carve limestone and fine woods that were then painted in bright colors. Hard stone, such as granite, was carved with pounders made of stone.

Complete the following activities.

1. Imagine that you are an ancient Egyptian artist. A wealthy nobleman has commissioned you to paint a mural in the central hall of his palace. The central hall is the heart of the residence and even though the walls were not usually covered with painted scenes as in the palaces, he wanted to break with tradition. Plan the mural carefully before you make the final copy. Be creative but follow the Egyptian stylized form. Make your final drawing on 11″ × 17″ paper.

2. Amulets were good luck charms worn by adults and children around their necks or wrists or tucked in the wrappings of mummies. An amulet could be shaped like an animal, bug, or a god. Make your version of an amulet from clay. Make a hole in the clay if you want to wear the amulet as a necklace. When the clay object is dry or fired, paint it in bright colors.

3. The scarab is a beetle that rolls up balls of dung in which to lay its eggs. The Egyptians believed that a giant scarab made the sun in the same way and then rolled it over the horizon and across the sky. The scarab is the symbol of rebirth. Both men and women wore jewelry and amulets shaped like scarabs. Create on paper a piece of jewelry (necklace, bracelet, ring, belt, collar) using the scarab design. Use colors to simulate gold, lapis lazuli, turquoise, amethyst, and other gemstones and colored glass. Label your drawing.

Mummies

It was a religious practice of the ancient Egyptians to supply the dead with a well-functioning body in the afterlife. Ancient Egyptians believed that everyone had a soul which was released from the body at the time of death. In order for the soul to rest at night, the body had to be preserved, or mummified. The embalming began with the extraction of the brain through the nostrils. Then an opening was cut in the side of the body and the insides were removed. The intestines, lungs, stomach, and liver were mummified separately and placed in containers called canopic jars. The body was packed with a salt called *natron* to dry it out. Then the body was wrapped in many yards of linen. Amulets and jewelry were placed between the layers of linen. A death mask, a portrait of the dead person, was placed on the mummy. The whole process was based on the strict rituals of the *Book of the Dead* and took about 70 days.

On the day of the funeral, the mummy and canopic chest traveled by barge to the site of the tomb. Priests, the family, and hired mourners followed the mummy to the door of the tomb where a priest performed a religious rite. The coffin was taken into the burial chamber and put in the outer coffin, or sarcophagus. The lid was sealed. The Egyptians believed the person's soul had by then arrived in the Judgment Hall of Osiris, to be weighed against a feather. If the two balanced, it meant he or she had led a good life.

1. Death masks were placed over the heads of the mummified pharaohs. Make a list of the ways that masks are used in our culture. Think about when masks are worn for sports, holidays, games, and parties.

2. Match the terms on the left with the descriptions.

   a. sarcophagus   _____ good luck charm

   b. canopic jars   _____ ritualistic rules for
                                             mummification

   c. embalm   _____ containers for organs

   d. amulet   _____ large outer coffin

   e. natron   _____ salt

   f. *Book of the Dead*   _____ prevent a body from decaying

3. On the back of this page, design a death mask fit for an Egyptian pharaoh.

FS-23226 Social Studies Made Simple • © Frank Schaffer Publications, Inc.

Spotlight on Giza

The biggest and the best pyramids are the ones at Giza. The Great Pyramid of Giza was built round 2550 BC by Khufu, probably the most powerful pharaoh ever to rule Egypt. The pyramid is made of about 2,300,000 blocks of solid limestone, each weighing about 2.5 tons. Scholars estimate that it took 100,000 men 20 years to build the Great Pyramid. Deep within the pyramid is a complex network of passages and dead-end chambers, escape and ventilation shafts, and a burial chamber lined with shiny red granite where Khufu's mummy was placed.

More than 80 Egyptian pyramids have survived for nearly 5,000 years. The building of a pyramid was a sacred undertaking. A pharaoh built a pyramid as the final resting place for his body. Building a pyramid required careful planning. A site was chosen on the west bank of the Nile. The site had to be close to the river so stones could be easily transported. The site needed a solid base of rock to support all of the massive stones. The site then had to be carefully leveled and all of the dimensions carefully calculated. Pyramids were expensive to build, and the people were taxed heavily to help pay for them. Industries grew up around the pyramids and included architects, builders, painters, carvers, and numerous craftworkers. By the time Tutankhamen ruled, the pyramids at Giza were more than a thousand years old, and the people of his time thought they were ancient wonders.

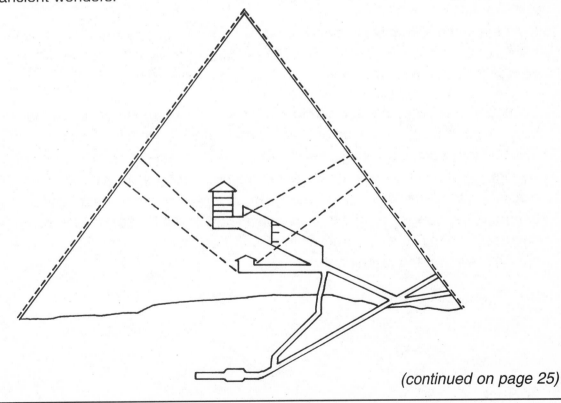

(continued on page 25)

Spotlight on Giza (continued)

The Great Sphinx

The great Egyptian sphinx is also located at Giza. A large stone sculpture with the head of a king or queen and the body of a lion, the sphinx is a symbol of royal power. Rows of sphinxes often guard the entrance to a temple. The Great Sphinx, created about 2500 BC for Pharaoh Khafre, was carved from a huge outcrop of limestone. It is 187 feet long and 66 feet high. It is the largest freestanding sculpture to survive from ancient times. The drifting sands buried it up to its neck for most of its history.

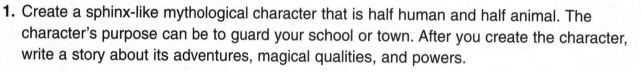

As early as 1400 BC, Thutmose IV attempted to restore it and to clear it from the sand. According to one historical record, Thutmose IV stopped his hunting party near the Sphinx. While he napped in its shade, the Sphinx appeared to him in a dream. The Sphinx prophesied that Thutmose IV would be made king if he freed the sphinx from the sand. Thutmose did free it, improved it with new limestone blocks, and painted it blue, yellow, and red. Ramses II also did extensive work on the Sphinx in 1279 BC. The sphinx was finally dug completely out of the desert sands in 1925.

1. Create a sphinx-like mythological character that is half human and half animal. The character's purpose can be to guard your school or town. After you create the character, write a story about its adventures, magical qualities, and powers.

2. In 1996, the second largest pyramid in Egypt, Khafre, was reopened to tourists. It had been closed to repair damage caused by humidity, the greatest threat to the pyramids. The humidity comes from sweat and exhaled water vapor from thousands of daily visitors. The humidity weakens the pyramids by drawing salt from their huge limestone blocks. Pretend that you were in charge of adding a historical attraction to the pyramid before it opened—a way that tourists could learn about Khafre and his burial place. You have decided to use a hologram of Khafre talking to the tourists. Decide what his message will be and write it here:

Name _____

Ancient Egyptian Gods

Egyptians had more than 700 gods. Only a small number were worshipped in the same place and at the same time. Most changed their character over the centuries. As new gods were accepted, they often blended with other gods. Temples were built for gods. A temple was the palace of the god, and priests would perform elaborate rituals and offer prayers and sacrifices to the god.

Below are the pictures of nine Egyptian gods with a short description of each. Study them carefully to see their characteristics, the symbols they hold, and the way they are dressed. Do research to find out the name of each god. Write the name on the line below each drawing.

 Son of Osiris; god of the sky

_____

 Brother of Isis; god of agriculture; ruler of the dead

_____

 Goddess of love, music and dance

_____

 Wife and sister of Osiris; mother of Horus

_____

 Goddess of joy and love; also goddess of war

_____

 God of writing and wisdom; also of learning and science

_____

 God of the dead

_____

 God of the sun; sailed across the heavens; considered king of gods

_____

 National god and patron of artists and craftsmen

_____

Kush

Time: 2000 BC–AD 350 (approximate)

Location: along the Nile River in what is now southern Egypt and northern Sudan

Significance: An ancient African civilization, Kush developed long-distance trade, its own writing system, and an iron-working industry.

WHERE IS KUSH?

`Class Activity`

Take your students on an imaginary airplane ride over the kingdom of Kush. First note that Kush is part of the region known as Nubia where the flight will begin. The plane takes off from Aswan and flies over the First Cataract along the Nile River. The cataracts are rapids and waterfalls that interrupted the course of the Nile six times. The border between Nubia and Egypt often fluctuated. Notice that the land along the Nile is less bountiful in this region than it is in Egypt. Follow the course of the Nile past the Second and Third Cataracts. Take a short break when your plane lands at the town of Napata, which was the first capital of Kush. As the plane takes off again and flies over the Fourth Cataract, you will enter the heart of the Kush kingdom. The plane flies over the city of Meroë which became Kush's second capital and a great cultural and trading center. This area had most of Kush's iron ore and was an iron-making center. The plane will land again at Khartoum near the southern border of the Kush empire. The city is also where the Blue Nile and White Nile converge. At this point, give each student an outline map that includes Egypt and the Sudan. Have them draw in the Nile River, the six cataracts, Napata, Meroë, Aswan, Khartoum, the Blue Nile, and the White Nile.

LOST ON THE DESERT

`Class Activity`

The kingdom of Kush was mostly desert. The largest desert in the kingdom was the Nubian Desert which was actually a part of the Sahara. Use the Sahara as a topic for a research project. Assign students or small groups of students a subtopic. For example, students can research climate, animal and bird life, plant life, the wadis and oases, erosion and environmental issues, travel on the desert, other great deserts of the world. As "desert experts," students should report to the class on their findings. Then ask each student to write a story based on the theme "lost in the Sahara." To make the story more factual, students should include as much of the information in the research reports as possible.

GIVE AND TAKE

Kush was of strategic importance to ancient Egypt. Egypt was especially interested in trading for elephant tusks, panther skins, gold, exotic animals, and ebony, the black wood from a hardwood tree that grows in the Nubian desert. Egyptian rulers kept moving their border further into Nubia and built forts and trading posts in the region. Kush was strongly influenced by Egyptian culture. Kushites copied Egyptian temples and pyramids, art, and even some of their gods.

Discuss with your class the cultural exchanges that go on among countries today. China warns her citizens about becoming too "westernized." France has a committee to keep foreign words out of the French language. In all parts of the world, tourists can find McDonalds and other American products, fashions, music, and even slang. Have students pretend they are Kushites opposed to so many Egyptian ideas coming into Kush. Have each student write an editorial for the *Nubian News* stating his or her complaints and the reasons for them.

KUSHITE PHARAOHS OF EGYPT

Over time, Egypt, weakened by civil wars and disorder, was open for conquest. In the eighth century BC, Kush conquered Egypt and established a vast empire extending from the Mediterranean to the modern Ethiopian border. For about a hundred years, the kings of Kush were also pharaohs of Egypt. Challenge your students to find out more about the Kush kings by researching Kashta, Piankhy (Piye), Shabaka, and Taharqa (Tirhaka). Have them include a paragraph on why Kush is considered an important ancient kingdom.

IRON ORE

Meroë was surrounded by deposits of iron ore and was the center of an iron smelting industry. Meroë may have been the source of the spread of iron casting techniques in ancient Africa. Iron was stronger than bronze and made excellent tools and weapons. Have students research the Iron Age and make a list of ancient civilizations and the years that iron was first used in them. Add a paragraph explaining how iron ore can be turned into iron that is then used for weapons.

THE IMPRESSIVE ABU SIMBEL

Two of the great temples built in Nubia were commissioned by an Egyptian pharaoh, Ramses II. He may have built such grand temples to impress and intimidate the Nubians who paid him tribute. The temples are at Abu Simbel and are dedicated to Ramses and his queen, Nefertari. The temples, carved 160 feet into the hillside, include huge statues of the king. Around his legs are sculpted his mother, one of his wives, and eight of his 140 children. Provide reference materials so that students can learn more about the design of Abu Simbel, the mystery of the light in the sanctuary, or the "drowning" of the temples in the 1960s. Students can report their findings to the class in the form of a news release, a picture page for a children's book, or in an oral presentation.

Temples and Pyramids

Near Napata, the first capital of Kush, the first Kushites built pyramids in the Egyptian style. The pyramids were filled with statuary and ritual items also based on Egyptian designs. The pyramids were slightly smaller than Egyptian pyramids, the mummies were put under the pyramids instead of inside them, and the sides of the pyramids were steeper. More than one hundred pyramids have been found in the Nubia region, but most have been badly plundered. Only one—at Meroë—the tomb of Queen Amanishakheto, who ruled Nubia in the first century BC, has survived without being robbed. Many gold bracelets, rings, pendants, and necklaces cut from sheets of solid gold were found in her burial chamber.

The best-preserved is King Aspelta's tomb at Nuri, near Napata. He is one of the first Nubian rulers to be buried in a coffin and a stone sarcophagus rather than on a bed. Also in the Nuri area are twenty large pyramids and fifty-three smaller ones built for queens. Near a site where four pharaohs were buried, archaeologists discovered a horse cemetery. In it were 24 horses buried standing upright and decorated with nets of cowrie shells and bronze beads.

Complete the following activities.

1. Although many Kushite rulers wore the double crown of the Egyptian pharaoh, some wore a crown with two sacred cobras. The cobra was also on the Egyptian crown. The cobra was placed on the front of the crown as a symbol of the king's right to rule. Write down three characteristics of the cobra that make it a good symbol for a pharaoh.

   _____   _____   _____

2. Pretend that you are the craftsman and goldsmith and have been commissioned to make a new crown for the king of Kush. It must incorporate a cobra in its design but can also include other animals and plants. Make your design here and explain how it represents the kingdom of Kush.

3. On a separate piece of paper, make cross sections of an Egyptian pyramid and a Kushite pyramid. Label at least three differences between the two.

Ancient India

Time: 2500 BC–AD 467

Location: initially the Indus Valley, spreading to the Ganges Valley, northern India, and the Deccan plateau in central India

Significance: The people of ancient India domesticated horses, invented the chariot, wrote the Vedas, devised a class system, and used the writing system called Sanskrit.

GREAT RIVER IDENTIFICATION

Class Activity

Early civilizations grew up along some of the major rivers of the world including the Euphrates, the Nile, and the Indus. Have students divide a piece of paper into three columns. Label the first column Nile River, the middle column Euphrates River, and the third Indus River. Then read the following list of places, animals, and cities. Students should write the items in the correct column. (The items can also be written on the board.) Challenge students to come up with more terms to add to their charts.

Nubia, Delta, Thebes, Harappa, water buffalo, tigers, Memphis, cataracts, crocodiles, Ur, Babylon, Persian Gulf, Mediterranean Sea, Sumer, Mohenjo-Daro, leopards, Ravi, modern Pakistan, modern Iraq, hippopotamus, rhinoceros, Punjab, Arabian Sea

RIVER DEVELOPMENT

Class Activity

The Indus River forms one of India's great river systems. Like the Nile and the Euphrates, the Indus River was an ideal place for people to settle. There were grasslands, large forests, ample wildlife, and an annual flooding of the river which provided fertile soil for farming. The river also provided transportation and helped spread new ideas. Ask your class to come up with several reasons why civilizations grew up along rivers. Find out if they can name rivers in North America where great cities developed. Do they think the reasons for growth of recent cities along rivers are the same as for those in ancient times?

THE AMAZING CITY OF HARAPPA

Class Activity

Harappa, India, was home to almost 40,000 people. At the center of the town was an artificial mound of earth covering about 16 acres. A huge citadel was built on the mound. A brick embankment forty-five feet thick at the base protected the citadel from erosion. Walls with towers and battlements protected it from invaders. To the north of the citadel, the great granary made from brick contained threshing floors, barracks for laborers, and loading platforms for grain. A set of furnaces may have been used for forging bronze. Below, the city spread out, its main streets linked by smaller lanes in grid fashion. Brick houses, craft shops, and restaurants lined the streets. Describe Harappa to your students. Ask them to draw plans of the city based on your description. Then refer to pictures of Harappa in reference and resource books. Have them make changes in their plans based on the pictures. Ask them which was easier to understand, the verbal or the visual description.

TRADE

Class Activity

People in the Indus valley traded for gold, copper, ivory, gemstones, turquoise, lapis lazuli, and cedar from Kashmir region and for teak from Punjab. They also traded in cotton because people of the Indus region were the first to make cotton cloth. Traders' caravans brought back steatite, alabaster, and a tarry bitumen that was used for waterproofing. In Afghanistan, Indus traders sought gold, silver, and perhaps tin. They imported jade from the Himalayas, lapis lazuli from Afghanistan, and turquoise from Persia. In addition to links between the cities, there were trade links by sea with the Persian Gulf and Mesopotamia. On an outline map, label the places where people from the Indus Valley traded and write the imports that came from each country or region.

ARYANS ARRIVE

Class Activity

The Aryans were nomadic herders who, over hundreds of years, left their homelands in the steppes of southern Russia and immigrated into the Indus Valley. They may have caused the collapse of the Indus Valley civilization. Ask students to think of reasons why people migrate. (Some might be natural disasters, economic hardships, invasions or war, a shortage of food, or free land.) Discuss the positive and negative aspects of the migrations of great numbers of people both on the country they are leaving and on the country to which they are migrating. What do students think are the fears and expectations of immigrants?

VEDAS

Group Activity

Aryans are known for developing an elaborate system of spiritual ideas in the form of hymns or poems called *Vedas*. Vedas were passed on orally from one generation to the next by priests who made certain that no changes crept in. Eventually they were written down; nearly all of the information that is known about the Aryans comes from the Vedas, which are the basis of the Hindu religion. Share some of the poems from the Vedas. Have small groups of students each prepare a choral reading of a poem.

CLASSES OF PEOPLE OR VARNAS

Class Activity

The Aryans and others classified people into groups: *brahmans*—priests and scholars; *kshatriyas*—warriors and rulers; *vaishyas*—farmers, traders, and business people; and *sudras*—servants and workers. Eventually, these groups developed subgroups called castes. A person was born within a caste and stayed there for a lifetime. During the Aryan Period, a fifth group emerged: the outcasts or untouchables, whose main occupations were the cremation of the dead and dirty, bloody, or menial jobs. The Indian Constitution of 1950 outlawed untouchability and gave the group full citizenship. A basic part of Hinduism is the caste system. Talk to your class about classifying people based on birth, economics, or education. What classes exist in the United States? Discuss the main differences between classes in the United States and the caste system of India. Are there any "classless" societies?

FS-23226 *Social Studies Made Simple* ■ © Frank Schaffer Publications, Inc.

CHANDRAGUPTA MAURYA

····· **Group Activity** ·····

Chandragupta Maurya, India's first emperor, was a military genius who founded the Mauryan Civilization (324–183 BC). At the height of his rule, 600,000 infantry, 30,000 cavalry, 9,000 war elephants, and 8,000 chariots were part of his army. Chandragupta Maurya ruled over people of diverse races, languages, religions, and cultures. Commerce and industry flourished. Artisans manufactured jewelry, perfumes, fine fabrics, leatherwork, pottery, and clothing. Trade flourished from the seaport towns. As Chandragupta grew older, he developed a deepening interest in Jainism, the "religion of the conquerors." Jains reinterpreted the basics of Hinduism. They believed that every living thing had a soul, and that killing any living thing was evil. Jains could not be farmers, since cultivating the soil would kill creatures living in the earth. According to Jainist tradition, Chandragupta abdicated his throne in 301 BC and entered a monastery where he slowly starved himself to death. As a research project, students can make their own "Mini-Encyclopedia of the World's Religions." Small groups can work on one religion and the entries can be bound together. Allow time for students to give oral presentations on religions.

GUPTA DYNASTY

······ **Class Activity** ······

Around AD 320, the Gupta Dynasty unified northern India and ruled over a prosperous country with law and justice, scientific advances, and achievements in the arts. Chandra Gupta II reigned around AD 376–415. He gave up warfare and concentrated on the arts of peace. Taxation was light. Serious crime was rare. Chandra Gupta gathered together poets, artists, musicians, and scientists and sponsored poetry and drama competitions. Organize the class into small groups and have each group create a poem, dramatic presentation, or musical presentation. After each group presents an entry, let the class vote on the best presentation.

SCIENCE

······ **Class Activity** ······

Indus Valley scholars in the sciences, medicine, and mathematics excelled in their fields. Many basic medical practices, compiled in a textbook from that time, are still in use today. Doctors encouraged cleanliness and understood the importance of the spinal cord and the workings of the nervous system. They could set bones and repair lost or injured noses, lips, and ears. In the fifth century, the great astronomer and mathematician Aryabhata stated that the earth was round, rotated on its axis, and revolved around the sun. It would be centuries before European astronomers would reach the same conclusions. The biggest impact, though, was in the field of mathematics. Mathematicians developed the system of number that we use today—the system with a zero, nine digits, and a decimal. They also worked with negative and abstract numbers. Tell students to choose one of these topics—the spinal cord and the nervous system; setting a broken bone; the earth and how it moves; zero and the decimal system; negative and abstract numbers—and prepare a three-minute instructive talk to be given in front of the class. The students should prepare a chart or diagram to use during the talk.

Hinduism

The Aryan Period

During the Aryan period in the Indus Valley, religion became more complicated. Not even the king was able to understand all the religious mysteries. Of the Aryan religion's 33 gods, Indra was one of the most important. He was the god of war and storms and carried a thunderbolt in his hand. In later times, when the Aryan's religion changed to Hinduism, Indra was replaced by Brahma, Vishnu, Shiva, and Krishna. Other Vedic gods were Varuna, the god of justice and king of universal order, and Yama, the god of death.

Dissatisfied with the religious rituals, religious thinkers began wandering the countryside. They lived like hermits seeking wisdom and truth. Many principles that ultimately became a part of Hindu doctrine were first expressed by these holy men. They taught that a search for truth was found through intuition and self-denial. The discipline of yoga prepared them for the search. They also introduced the idea of transmigration of souls (the endless cycle of death and rebirth), karma (a person's good or bad deeds results in a reward or punishment), and dhama (righteous living or moral duty).

The Gupta Dynasty

During the Gupta dynasty, two great religions, Buddhism and Hinduism, existed side by side. Hinduism is considered by most authorities to be more a way of life than a religion, so the two religions were not in direct conflict. Hinduism is not based on a central figure like the Buddha or Jesus. Instead Hinduism binds people together with a set of strongly held common beliefs. Hindus do not have a single holy book like the Bible or Koran, but instead have many sacred writings.

Polytheism

The Hindus worship many gods (polytheism). They recognize one god, Brahman, as supreme, but he is so complex that mortal people cannot comprehend him. Three important deities, Brahma, the creator; Vishnu, the preserver of the universe; and Shiva, the destroyer and god of death are part of this complex deity. Krishna, an incarnation of Vishnu, is strong and brave and well loved by the people. Worshippers created special rituals for these gods. Ornately carved sculptures depicting episodes from the lives of the gods adorned large temples dedicated to them.

(continued on page 34)

FS-23226 Social Studies Made Simple ■ © Frank Schaffer Publications, Inc.

Hindusim *(continued)*

Use an encyclopedia or other books and do research on early religions. Use the information from your studies and your research to compare some of the world's religions. Write your findings on the following chart:

	Central Figure(s)	Holy Book or Writings	Practiced in These Countries
Christianity			
Hinduism			
Judaism			
Buddhism			

(continued on page 35)

Hindusim *(continued)*

Identify the Hindu gods by writing the name of each on the line provided.

_____

the creator. Once thought the greatest of the gods because he set the universe in motion. From his four heads sprang the Vedas.

the preserver of the universe and the ultimate source of everything that is. He worked constantly for the good of the world. This is why he incarnated nine times when the world was in great danger of being destroyed.

_____

the best loved of all Vishnu's incarnations. He loved humanity and was very human and naughty as a child, playing all sorts of pranks.

god of death and time. He was also the universal teacher. He sat high up in the Himalayas, deep in meditation that maintained the world. He became Lord of the Dance and was the inventor of 108 different types of dances.

FS-23226 Social Studies Made Simple ▪ © Frank Schaffer Publications, Inc.

Elephants

The herds of elephants ridden by armed Indian warriors were terrifying! The Indians were skilled at capturing wild elephants and training them for battle. They used soothing music to pacify the beasts and rewarded them with food for good behavior. Before going into battle, the elephants were painted with bright colors and their tusks were tipped with metal spikes. They wore leather armor and huge bronze bells around their necks. It was also common that the elephants were given large quantities of rice wine to increase their aggressiveness. Elephants carried a driver and several soldiers equipped with shields and spears. The army also had a cavalry and foot soldiers. The elephants marched at the head of the army, breaking the enemy's ranks, smashing defenses, and causing fear in the enemy.

Complete the following activities.

1. Imagine that you have been granted permission to accompany the king's army on a peace mission to a neighboring kingdom. Even though the army is outfitted for battle, it is bringing chests of treasures as gifts. You will be traveling at the back of the army with the family members, but you will have access to all of the officers and soldiers, elephant trainers, veterinarians, and cooks. This is an amazing opportunity for you to actually talk to these people and record their thoughts. Put the results of your interviews in the form of a radio documentary, a factual story for a newspaper or magazine, or a creative story for a literary magazine. Where appropriate, include illustrations.

2. Write a myth explaining how elephants got their trunks.

3. Learn about Ganesha, the elephant-headed god who brings prosperity to those who worship him. Write a story about Ganesha, a young, courageous child, and a cave of treasure.

Ancient Israel

Time: 2000 BC–AD 73

Location: encompassed the land that is now called Israel and parts of Jordan and Syria

Significance: origin of two of the world religions, Judaism, Christianity; origin of one all-powerful God; origin of much of western law.

KEEPING RECORDS

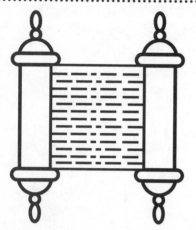

The Torah (first five books of the Old Testament), a record of the Jewish people, is one of the first written histories of an ancient people. The Torah's main purpose was religious, but it also included customs, laws, and history. Most historians use the Torah along with other sources such as archaeological evidence to get a clear picture of this time and place. Discuss with your class the advantages of using a variety of resources to learn about an event or group of people. Ask students what problems might come from using only one source. Divide your class into three groups. Have the first group pretend they are colonists during the American Revolutionary War. Tell the second group they are British soldiers in the war and tell the third group they are colonists sympathetic to the British. Have students in each group write a short news story about the war for the *Colonial Gazette.* Compare the stories. If only one viewpoint were published, what impression of the war would the readers have? As an additional activity, have students tell how their own lives have been documented. Have them make lists of all the ways that someone studying their lives 1,000 years from now would know what they were like and what they did.

UNDERSTANDING THE BIBLE

The word *Bible* is derived from the Greek *biblia,* meaning "books," and refers to the sacred writings of Judaism and Christianity. The *Bible* consists of two parts. The first, called the Old Testament, is the sacred writings of the Jewish people and was written originally in Hebrew. The second part, the New Testament, was composed in Greek and records the story of Jesus and the beginnings of Christianity. The Bible has been translated into more than 1,500 languages and is the most widely distributed book in the world. Instruct students to find other words in a dictionary with the root "biblia." Bring into class several versions of the Bible including the Hebrew Scriptures. After students have had a chance to compare the books, have them answer these questions: What are the differences and similarities between the Christian and the Jewish versions of the *Bible?* What are some kinds of variations in the translations of *Bibles?* What does "literal interpretation" of the *Bible* mean? Define these words: *Torah, Old Testament, New Testament, Apocrypha,* and *scriptures.* How has the *Bible* influenced literature and the arts? Have research materials available.

CONNECTIONS BETWEEN
MESOPOTAMIA AND ANCIENT ISRAEL

Class Activity

One group of people living in Mesopotamia around 1900 BC was a tribe of semi-nomadic herdsmen. One of them, Abraham, was soon to become the first leader of the Israelite nation and the founder of Judaism. Abraham was born at Ur in Chaldea. God commanded him to move to Canaan, the part of Syria and Palestine lying between the Mediterranean Sea and the Jordan River. Abraham obeyed, took his flocks and herds, and lived as a nomadic chieftain in accordance with a contract, or covenant, with God. Have your class make a list of synonyms for "covenant." Help them locate on a map the places where Abraham lived and where he went. Have your students discuss whether or not they have ever made an agreement with someone. What would have happened if one of the parties broke the agreement?

THREE RELIGIONS

Class Activity

Abraham became the father of the Israelite people, but he is honored in three different religions. Jewish tradition stresses his monotheism. Christians see him as a model for the man of faith and recognize him as their spiritual ancestor. Muslims accept him as an ancestor of the Arabs through Ishmael, his son. Have students write Abraham at the top of a piece of paper. Underneath have them write Judaism, Christianity, and Islam. Under the religions, students should write the religions relationship to Abraham and some other similarities between the religions. Tell where the three religions are practiced today. Have students work in small groups to research Islam. Have the groups gather pictures and magazine articles, make maps, or create something that symbolizes Islam and turn the information into a bulletin board.

THE HEBREW CALENDAR

Class Activity

The Hebrew calendar in use today begins at the Creation, which is calculated to have occurred 3,760 years before the Christian era. The week consists of seven days, ending with the Sabbath, Saturday; the year consists of 12 lunar months which are alternately 29 and 30 days long. Because a year is some 11 days longer than 12 lunar months, a 13th month is added seven times during every 19-year cycle. Contact a synagogue or a family in your school to find out if you can borrow a Hebrew calendar. Have students calculate the present year.

LAWS AND TEN COMMANDMENTS

Class Activity

Although many laws in the Torah were similar to those of other nations in the region, some unique laws, such as those in the Ten Commandments, are also written in the Torah. Many of these laws have a high ethical content. Laws are guidelines that groups of people use to govern themselves. Discuss some of these questions with your class: Who makes the laws in our society? What makes a good law? What is an unfair law? Have students work in small groups to come up with five good laws for the classroom. Have each group read its laws and then vote on those that they think are the five best.

BEING THE FIRST

When the Hebrews returned to Israel from Egypt, they found that the Canaanites had occupied their Promised Land. After a long series of battles, the Hebrews gained control of most of the hill country. In Hebrew society, a judge was usually chosen as a leader. After the battle, the judge went back into the ranks of the people. The Israelites soon realized they needed a stronger leader to unite them. The first choice was Saul who was a military expert known for his bravery. As king, he enjoyed considerable initial success and was responsible for the strength and cohesion of the Hebrew nation. But Saul was envious of the brilliant young commander David, and his jealousy began to destroy his judgment. He met with disastrous defeat on Mount Gilboa. He killed himself rather than accept capture. Discuss with students what it must be like to be the "first" of anything (first woman, first black, first on the moon, first child)? Tell your class to imagine that the school board decided to have someone from your class run the school district. Talk about the pressures, problems, and expectations placed on that student. What could the rest of the class do to help?

CAPTURING JERUSALEM

David was the second king of Israel. He brought together all the tribes of Israel and governed for 40 years. David realized that Jerusalem would be the perfect capital for a united kingdom, but Jerusalem was a walled city with good defenses and well-armed soldiers. David sent spies into Jerusalem. The city's weak spot, the spies reported, was the water supply. Scouts went into the water tunnel, climbed the shaft that brought water into Jerusalem, and opened a city gate to allow the rest of the Israeli army inside. David led a great march into Jerusalem. The Ark of the Covenant was carried into the city and given a permanent home. Jerusalem became the political and religious center for all the tribes. Have students complete a storyboard, including captions and illustrations, that might be used to film a television documentary about the capture of Jerusalem.

SOLOMON AND THE FIRST TEMPLE

When David died in 961 BC, Solomon, David's son, came to power. Solomon constructed the famous temple in Jerusalem, the center of religious life for the Israelites. To build the temple, 30,000 laborers cut cedar logs in Lebanon. One hundred fifty thousand workmen cut out the limestone for stone blocks. Expeditions went to Africa for ivory and to India for gold. The temple lasted nearly 400 years, but eventually its riches were carried off by the Babylonians in 586 BC. Later Jerusalem's wall was rebuilt, but when the Roman general Titus destroyed Jerusalem, he burned the temple. All that remained was the western wall. For centuries Jews called this site the Wailing Wall. Today it is known as the Western Wall. Have students do a research project on the Temple in Jerusalem. Have them use travel books to learn what tourists see today when they visit the temple. Use current newspapers and magazines to learn about political, archaeological, and cultural happenings around the temple area. Ask them to write an editorial on whether they think the temple should be rebuilt.

FS-23226 Social Studies Made Simple ▪ © Frank Schaffer Publications, Inc.

BEGINNING OF CHRISTIANITY

Class Activity

After the Romans captured Israel, many Jews hoped that one day Israel would again be an independent nation. They searched for a leader who would free them from foreign rule. The idea that a messiah, or "anointed one," would someday come and free the people became a part of the Jewish belief. During the Roman occupation of Israel, Jesus was born in Bethlehem (about 5 BC). Many believed that Jesus was the messiah, but most of the Jews did not. They saw him as a troublemaker, as did the Romans. In AD 33, Jesus was arrested for treason against Rome and sentenced to death by crucifixion.

Some of Jesus' followers continued to believe in his teachings. They believed that Jesus was resurrected and that the Kingdom of God was coming soon. These followers became the early Christians. They spread Jesus' teachings and the story of his life far beyond Israel. Using art books, have students choose their favorite piece of classical art based on the life of Jesus and make a report on the artist and the meaning of the work. Have students name the famous cathedrals erected for the worship of Jesus. Compare the architecture of a cathedral to a Buddhist temple or a Jewish synagogue. Students can make a chart comparing Judaism and Christianity. Include symbols of each (for example, the fish, cross, star of David, menorah), holy cities, holy books, places of worship, religious holidays and celebrations, names of religious leaders, and important historical figures.

BIBLICAL TERMS FOUND IN LITERATURE

Class Activity

Have students define these words in modern terms and then tell their Biblical significance:

apocalypse	a Judas
babel	land of milk and honey
chapter and verse	manna from heaven
having a cross to bear	salt of the earth
the road to Damascus	turn the other cheek
a David and Goliath situation	shibboleth
a doubting Thomas	
a good Samaritan	
as patient as Job	

Moses

Moses was born in Egypt, where the Hebrews were living as slaves of the Egyptians. When Moses was an infant, the pharaoh ordered all male children of the Hebrews slain. Moses' mother placed him in a reed basket and hid him in a marsh. He was found by the Pharaoh's daughter, who adopted him. As an adult, Moses killed an Egyptian who was beating a Hebrew. To escape punishment, Moses went into exile.

One day, God spoke to Moses from a burning bush and commanded him to return to Egypt to lead the Hebrews out of slavery. Moses returned to Egypt to confront the pharaoh. After a long struggle involving ten plagues and culminating in the slaying of the firstborn of the Egyptians, the pharaoh permitted the Hebrews to leave. Then the pharaoh changed his mind and sent an army to force the Hebrews to return. God drowned the pursuing Egyptians in the Red Sea, and Moses led the Hebrews to the sacred mountain—named Sinai in one source, Horeb in another. There God appeared to them in a frightening display of thunder and lightning. Moses went up into the mountains and returned with the Ten Commandments. The Old Testament tells of many conflicts between Moses and the people during this time. The most dramatic one concerned the Golden Calf set up by Moses' brother Aaron while Moses was on Mount Sinai. When Moses saw the idol, he was enraged and destroyed it. The forty-year journey back to Canaan became known as the Exodus. Moses died within sight of the Promised Land.

Complete the following activities.

1. Use the Book of Exodus in the Bible to find and list the ten plagues that God inflicted on Egypt before the pharaoh finally allowed Moses to lead the Hebrews out of Egypt.

2. The books of Exodus through Deuteronomy in the Bible are the only available sources for details about Moses' life. No Egyptian documents from that time mention him. Some scholars feel that there was ample time for legends to be built up around Moses. Read more about Moses and hypothesize what some of the legends might be.

3. The story of the baby Moses in the reed basket on the Nile is a typical legend about a famous man's childhood. A similar story is told about Sargon, king of Akkad (c. 2350 BC). Write your own story, using an imaginary hero who begins his life hidden in a basket in a river.

Spotlight on the Dead Sea Scrolls

In 1947, a Bedouin shepherd was exploring a cave in Qumran, near the Dead Sea, when he spotted some ancient scrolls. After archaeologists and linguists studied the scrolls, they were convinced that the Essenes, one of the Jewish sects that emerged around the time of Jesus, had hidden the scrolls there. Most scientists now think that the group moved to Qumran around 150–100 BC after a conflict with the ruling high priests in Jerusalem.

The Essenes considered themselves to be the true Israel, zealously obeying biblical law as interpreted by Essene leaders. Some 500 scrolls attributed to the Essenes date from about 250 BC to AD 70. They contain hymns, psalms, prayers, and all of the books of the Old Testament except Esther. One of the scrolls is called the War Scroll because it describes the final, apocalyptic battle of good against evil. The Temple Scroll describes an ideal Jerusalem Temple and laws for a sanctified people.

Although they had been preserved in dry caves for almost 2,000 years, all the scrolls showed some damage. Infrared photography and a variety of other scientific techniques were used to decipher the writing. The largest and best preserved scrolls were made available to scholars. However, many of the manuscripts had broken into hundreds of small parts that had to be pieced together. An international team of scholars divided the work, but even after 40 years, many of the texts still had not been published. To help researchers solve this problem, the Huntington Library of San Marino, California, photographed the unpublished texts and made them available to the public.

Answer the following questions based on the reading.

1. Write down three reasons why the discovery of the Dead Sea Scrolls is considered so important by archaeologists, historians, and religious scholars.

   _____

   _____

   _____

2. The Dead Sea is located in the Dead Sea Rift, a deep break in the earth's crust. As the geological expert on the Dead Sea, you are frequently asked questions about the area. Use your resource materials to find answers to the following questions:

   a. What happens along the Dead Sea Rift?

   b. What rivers flow into the Dead Sea?

FS-23226 Social Studies Made Simple ■ © Frank Schaffer Publications, Inc.

Ancient China

Time: 4500 BC–AD 195

Location: the general area of modern China today

Significance: longest, continuous civilization; many important inventions

Art Project

Geography

Making a relief map is probably one of the best ways to illustrate that China is a huge country with tremendous physical barriers. Have students make individual relief maps using a base of tagboard. Use papier-mâché to build up the features. Allow it to dry between layers. When the map is thoroughly dry, paint each region a different color. Be sure to include these physical features: Chang Jiang (Yangtze), Huang He, Himalayas, Gobi Desert, Takla Makan Desert, Turpan (Turfan) Depression, Pearl River, Plateau of Tibet (Tibetan Highlands), Tian Shan, Kunlun Shan Mongolian steppes, and major cities Beijing, Guilin, Xi'ian, Shanghai, Chang'du, and Guangzhou.

ISOLATION

Class Activity

Mountains, deserts, and bodies of water helped isolate China from the rest of the world. Also, China considered itself the center of the universe, and resisted foreign influences. Although complete isolation was impossible, access to foreigners was limited, even along the Silk Road and in port cities. This isolation allowed Chinese beliefs, traditions, and political practices to remain essentially unchanged for more than 2,000 years. Discuss the cultural effects of isolation. How would things be different if we had no contact with foreign countries?

Isolation has occurred in the United States, too, in some parts of Appalachia. Experts found that certain aspects of language, songs, traditions, and other things remained unchanged over many years. Have students form small groups that will take the role of city councils who must follow the voice of the electorate and cut off an imagined city from all foreign influences. What are the areas that they need to focus on? (Start with language, food, products, media.) How will they isolate their city? Do students think they will enjoy living in this isolated city?

CONNECTION TO OTHER RIVERS

Class Activity

Trace the route of the Huang He. In a chart, have students compare the Huang He to the Nile, Indus, and Euphrates Rivers. Some categories on the chart can be source, influences on early civilizations, water control methods, problems, early agricultural methods.

DYNASTIES—WHAT ARE THEY?

Group Activity

A dynasty is the succession of rulers from the same family or line. Most dynasties used military force to seize control of a country. By naming himself emperor, and by passing the leadership on to his eldest son or closest relative, conquerers created dynasties that endured for up to three centuries. Some important dynasies in China were Qin, Han, Sui, Tang, Song, Yuan, Ming, and Qing. Have small groups research a dynasty. On 8½″ × 11″ paper, students can write the highlights of the dynasty. Add pictures and Chinese decorations. Papers can be taped together for a continuous time line.

EMERGENCE OF WRITING/ ANCESTOR WORSHIP

Class Activity

The Shang dynasty (1766–1122 BC) is the first dynasty about which historians have reliable information, probably because the first Chinese writing emerged during the Shang dynasty. The writing was seen on oracle bones. These were animal bones or tortoise shells on which questions to ancestor spirits and the gods were carved. According to some experts, the religious leaders heated the bones and the cracks that appeared were interpreted as "answers" to questions. Then the questions and answers were etched onto the bone. The oracle bones record the history of the Shang dynasty and give the names of its rulers. Have students make an outline of an oracle bone on a piece of 8½″ × 11″ paper. Within the outline, students can write five or six questions that they would want to ask their ancestors. On the back of the "oracle bone," students should write the hypothetical answers that their ancestors might have given.

ANYANG CITY'S TOMBS

Class Activity

From 1400 BC, Anyang was the capital of the Shang dynasty. For a long time, some scholars considered the Shang culture mythical. Then in 1928, the richest repository of artifacts of the Shang dynasty was discovered under the modern city of Anyang. Archaeological evidence showed a highly developed culture distinguished by a centralized political structure, great artistry in bronze, a writing system still in use today, an agricultural economy, and armies of thousands whose commanders rode in chariots. Discuss with students why tomb findings are so important to historians and archaeologists. On a large piece of paper, have students design a modern tomb that contains two items that tell about twentieth century in the following categories: food, transportation, religion, writing, household items, politics, and the arts. Each item should be labeled. Students can share "tombs" with the rest of the class.

GROWTH OF ZHOU DYNASTY (1122–221 BC)

When the Zhou gained power from the Shang dynasty, they took over a kingdom whose center was the Huang He (Yellow River) and its tributaries. Five centuries later, civilized China extended from Mongolia to well south of the Chang Jiang (Yangtze). As the Zhou dynasty began to decline in the eighth century BC, the Chinese world splintered into hundreds of states. Armies grew larger, and foot soldiers began to be used more than the elite corps of charioteers. Soldiers used double-edged swords of bronze or forged iron, and many carried a deadly weapon invented in China: the crossbow. Crossbows made chariots less effective because their arrows or pellets could be fired at the enemy from a safe distance.

The art of fighting on horseback was adopted, and before long cavalry units became standard across China. Battles went from brief chariot duels to long struggles involving tens of thousands of soldiers. At the battle of Chang Ping in 260 BC, more than a half million soldiers died. Yet it was also a period of great intellectual achievement, which produced the oldest surviving Chinese literature and three important schools of philosophy: Confucianism, Daoism, and Legalism. Some students may want to investigate the invention of the crossbow and how it changed warfare in China. They can write a story about charioteers who must adapt to being part of a huge army of soldiers on foot or horseback. Discuss with students the contradiction between increased warfare and the growth of culture and intellectual achievements.

LEGALISM—GOOD OR BAD?

Shi Huangdi, the king of the western state of Qin, defeated the warlords in all the other states and turned China into an empire. The emperor and his chief minister, Li Si, were disciples of a doctrine called *legalism*. It held that people could be controlled through strict laws and severe punishments. The emperor was quick to suppress criticism, especially from scholars who opposed the precepts of legalism. Those guilty of the most serious offenses were beheaded, chopped in half at the waist, or boiled in an enormous caldron. Legalist principles contrasted with the more humane teachings of Confucius. After students learn about legalism and the teachings of Confucius, have them present a "meeting of the minds" with Shi Huangdi and Confucius in a discussion of whose philosophy is most correct. This exercise can be done in small groups or with different sets of students role-playing Shi Huangdi and Confucius. A mediator can help the students find common ground and keep the discussion moving.

STANDARDIZATION OF CHINESE SCRIPT

One of the first things Shi Huangdi did to unite the country was to standardize the form of thousands of written Chinese characters. Have students discuss why in a country with many cultural and regional differences, it is important for government and commerce that people be able to communicate accurately with each other. Have them do research to find out why European countries are trying to unite in a common money system. Which countries do not want to see this happen, and what are their reasons?

OTHER REFORMS

Shi Huangdi standardized the system of weights and measures and commissioned a network of roads. The roads, more than 4,000 miles of them, radiated from the capital like wheel spokes. China's road network had 500 more miles of roads than that of the Romans, built 350 years later. Shi Huangdi decreed that all the wheels of carts and wagons using the roads should be the same distance apart, with uniform axle length. The decree meant that the ruts worn into the dirt were standardized, making travel quicker and safer. Have students make a list of the things that unify the United States today. Are there things within our society where standardization has not been achieved? Have students imagine that each of the states has a different money system, a different language, and a different measuring system. Ask students how would this complicate their lives if they were owners of an ice cream company that sold ice cream cakes to all 50 states.

JUDGING SHI HUANGDI

Shi Huangdi had a harsh and cruel side. He levied high taxes that led to widespread suffering and starvation. He burned books that criticized the times. Those who possessed copies of the Confucian Book of Odes had to give them up for burning. The only books that were spared were books on medicine, pharmacy, divination, agriculture, and forestry. Shi Huangdi had 460 scholars put to death—actually buried alive—because they could not find the elixir of life and the key to immortality. Different historians frequently express at least two different opinions of Shi Huangdi. Some think that he was cruel and unjust. Others admire him for his vision, strength, and ability to unify the country. Organize a debate on these issues. Students can role-play by having one student take the part of Shi Huangdi and other students act as judges. Question the emperor on some of his accomplishments and his "crimes." Discuss the qualities of a good leader. Did Shi Huangdi possess these qualities? Would a good leader today necessarily be a good leader during the Qin dynasty? Why might standards be different?

EATING LIKE AN EMPEROR

Poems, archaeological finds, and written histories list foods available in the Qin dynasty. Some of them include 46 different vegetables, dogs, pigs, cattle, sheep, goats, chickens, geese, pheasants, quail, carp, turtles, frogs, snails, soybeans, wheat, and millet. There are specific recipes for ribs of ox, stewed turtle, roast kid with yam sauce, flesh of the great crane, fried honey-cakes of rice flour, plump orioles, pigeons with broth, dog cooked in bitter herbs, salad of artemisia with stewed magpie, and green goose. Instruct students to imagine that they are owners of the Emperor's Eatery Catering Service. They must prepare a menu for a rich person's birthday party. Tell students to use flowery, descriptive language to name and describe each menu item, and to end the menu with a delicious and unusual birthday cake surprise.

DRAGON

Good and noble Chinese dragons are thought to bring good luck. During the Han dynasty, dragons became the official symbol of the emperor and represented his godly power. Chinese dragons may be wild and temperamental, but they are never evil. They symbolize the life-giving force of water; inhabit rivers, lakes, and seas; and hide in rain clouds. The Chinese dragon embodies wisdom, strength, and goodness. People believed the dragon brought happiness and good fortune. The dragon was often a part of the generous spirit that prevailed at the New Year's festival. Ask students to write and illustrate a story about a Chinese dragon, a princess, a task that she must perform, and a great rainstorm. Share the stories with the class.

SILK FOR SALE

moth laying eggs

caterpillar

The Chinese have raised silkworms silk since the Neolithic period, but during the Shang dynasty, the production of silk increased and silk became increasing desirable. To help students understand the advantages of silk, ask them to imagine that they are advertising executives who are magically transported back in time. Have students create a poster, billboard, or magazine ad announcing a new store dealing in silk clothing for the nobility. Highlight the benefits of silk: it looks delicate, even though it has very strong fibers; it is lightweight but retains warmth; it is a good insulator and the coolest of hot-weather fabrics; it can absorb moisture without feeling wet; it is easy to dye; and it is resistant to fire.

SMUGGLING OUT SILK SECRETS

The process of making silk was such a well-kept secret for hundreds of years that experts thought the fabric was created by magic. Eventually, silkworm eggs were smuggled out of China along the Silk Road. Soon rival silkworm industries sprang up in other parts of the world. According to some stories, around 400 AD a Chinese princess, on her way to marry a prince in a far-off land, smuggled silkworm eggs out of China. Other stories claim that traders put the eggs in pieces of bamboo to hide them when they traveled along the Silk Road. Tell students to write their own version of the smuggling. The story should be in the form of a newspaper article beginning with a "Dateline: Silk Road. It has just been learned that the source of silk is worms!"

SILK ROAD—GEOGRAPHY

For 4,000 years, the Silk Road was the main highway from China to the Roman Empire. The road has been used by the Shang dynasty but did not become "famous" until much later. Traders, pilgrims, soldiers, adventurers, and refugees traveled the route carrying silk, porcelain, spices, tea, flowers, and foods. Because of the dangers and high cost of carrying trade goods, only items of great value traveled the Silk Road. Have students write a story from the viewpoint of a trader on the Silk Road. Include information about the road—physical features, items that are being transported, fellow travelers, and dangers encountered.

FS-23226 Social Studies Made Simple ▪ © Frank Schaffer Publications, Inc.

BUDDHA

The Buddhist religion came to China from India along the Silk Road around AD 100. The founder of Buddhism was Siddhartha Gautama, called Buddha or "the Enlightened One." The son of a wealthy tribal lord, Buddha rebelled against his life of luxury and privilege as he grew older. Wandering as a monk for six years, he searched for peace and serenity. Eventually, enlightenment came to him, and he spent the rest of his life preaching what is called the "Middle Way," a path that avoids extremes. He preached that the misery humans experienced would be endless unless people stopped thinking only of themselves and their earthly desires. By practicing the Middle Way, a person can achieve nirvana, a state of freedom from the perpetual cycle of birth, suffering, death, and rebirth (reincarnation). The stories, or levels, of buildings called pagodas represent different levels of Buddhist "heaven" and are separated by overhanging, curled, roofs. China has about 2,000 pagodas. Have students look at reference books illustrating different types of pagodas. Then have them draw a pagoda in which each story represents an aspect of their lives. The carvings and additions to each story should help indicate what it represents.

MEETING RELIGIONS' FOUNDERS

The Silk Road was also an avenue for the exchange of ideas. Some of the most fundamental ideas and technologies in the world, including writing, the wheel, weaving, agricultural methods, and the world's great religions, traveled along this highway. Tell students to imagine that they have been given the power to call a meeting of the founders of the world's great religions (include the Buddha, Mohammed, Abraham, Jesus, a Hindu religious leader, and any others that they want to include). Assign one founder to each group and have the group research and create a list of questions for "their founders." Have the class discuss how each founder would answer the questions.

GRAND CANAL

Shi Huangdi built and used some canals to transport supplies to the armies and to bring water to fields. Under the Sui dynasty, however, rulers started working on the single most unifying link between China's north and south—the Grand Canal. More people worked on the Grand Canal than on the Great Wall. The Grand Canal eventually connected several great river systems, including the Chang Jiang (Yangtze), Huang He, and the Huai. The canal has since been celebrated as the longest man-made waterway on earth. On a map, students should locate China's Grand Canal and other great canals including the Erie Canal, Panama Canal, Suez Canal, the Kiel Canal, and the Marne-Rhine Canal. Discuss with your class the reasons for canal building and how canals have helped transportation and communication. Have students write about an imaginary trip down the Grand Canal during Sui times, describing life along the canal and the regional changes that they see. Encourage them to provide illustrations.

Two Great Philosophers

CONFUCIANISM

Confucius was born into a noble family that had lost its money at a time when China was in chaos and warfare raged among many feudal states. He was orphaned while he was still a child but gained an education, became a student of history, and held an influential government post. As a protest against the emperor's misrule, Confucius resigned to become a wandering scholar and teacher. He was China's first professional educator. He believed that the early years of the Zhou were golden years of social harmony. Most of his teaching was not religious. His system of ethics demanded strong moral principles, or a code of behavior that focused on the relationships between ruler and those ruled, father and son, husband and wife, older and younger brothers, and friend and friend. Following the death of Confucius, his followers collected his teachings into a group of books called the *Five Classics.* In 124 BC, the government established the Imperial University to educate future government officials in Confucian ideals. Confucianism became the official state philosophy.

Lao Tzu is believed to have been the founder of Taoism. As a librarian of a very wealthy prince, he became disillusioned by the decadence of court life, left the palace, and traveled extensively throughout China. Lao Tzu believed that people should live simply in harmony with nature. He disagreed with Confucius because he did not believe in regulations. Taoists often withdraw from public life because they believe involvement with government or groups conflicts with a life of inner reflection. Taoists thought it was possible

to discover the elixir of life and become immortal. Taoist monks offered emperors mysterious concoctions as the secret of immortality. Many consider Taoism to be China's only organized, indigenous religion.

Choose one of these quotations from Confucius, put the idea into your own words, and make a poster with an illustration to show the idea graphically.

- He who speaks without modesty will find it difficult to make his words good.
- Recompense injury with justice, and recompense kindness with kindness.
- What you do not want done to yourself, do not do to others.
- The people may be made to follow a path of action, but they may not be made to understand it.

Choose one of the quotations from Lao Tzu and use it as a basis for a short essay.

- A journey of a thousand miles must begin with a single step.
- To know what you do not know is the best. To pretend to know when you do not know is a disease.
- He who knows others is wise; He who knows himself is enlightened.

Name _____

The Great Wall

Of all his accomplishments, Emperor Shi Huangdi is most remembered for the Great Wall. The wall, a 2,600-mile barrier, was built to stop nomads from sweeping down and raiding settlements in northern China. The oldest portions of the wall date back to 770–476 BC and were eventually joined into one long barrier by Shi Huangdi around 221 BC. Meng Tian was the army general in charge of the building project. He recruited millions of conscripted laborers and convicts to work on the wall, fight the "barbarians," and construct roads. The task took 10 years. The contours of land changed along the Wall's course, and natural obstacles had to be removed by hand or bypassed. As the wall grew, supply routes became longer. So many people died constructing the wall that it is sometimes called the world's largest cemetery or the "Wall of Tears." The Wall gave China a definite border and defined the country. Today it is a symbol of the longevity of the Chinese empire.

Complete the following activities.

1. Define these terms:

conscript _____

dynasty _____

nomads _____

2. Hundreds of myths and legends are told about the building of the Great Wall. One legend tells the story of the emperor's magical black horse with a red mane and eyes that glowed in the dark. The horse dredged out the earth with his saddle dragging behind him. The workmen followed his course across deserts, up mountains, and into valleys. This journey accounts for the Wall's meandering route across China. Embellish this legend by supplying the details and descriptions. To add more excitement to the legend, add a dragon or a magical demon. Illustrate your legend with drawings.

Spotlight on the Terra-Cotta Warriors

The first emperor of China, Shi Huangdi, spent a good portion of his reign searching for elixir of life to ensure his immortality. Ironically, he also prepared for his death by building an elaborate burial complex near the modern city of Xi'an. His tomb appears to be an ordinary hill, but inside the hill is a vast underground palace. The main room has a domed ceiling studded with gems representing stars. Protective mazes full of booby traps surround this chamber.

Football field-sized pits containing almost 8,000 life-sized terra-cotta infantrymen, officers, archers, and chariots with charioteers surround the tomb. Most of the soldiers wear long, double-layered tunics, leggings, and square-toed footwear. The hairstyles are elaborate. Each is fashioned individually and every strand of hair is visible. Nearly 700,000 workers spent 36 years constructing the figures. The clay soldiers were painted and placed fifteen feet underground standing in battle formation ready to guard the emperor's tomb. A wooden roof covered with dirt protected the clay army.

Complete the following activities.

1. When archaeologists excavated the site of the terra-cotta warriors, they discovered that each Chinese soldier had a different face. Archaeologists believe that each clay statue is a replica of an actual soldier. Imagine that you are one of the archaeologists who uncovered the army of soldiers. Write a diary entry explaining your feelings as you come face to face with the warriors. Describe one of the soldiers. State what you think is the most important aspect of this discovery.

2. Tourists can visit the site of the terra-cotta warriors. In fact, it has become one of the most popular tourist stops in China. Fortunately, the Chinese government has built a protective exhibition hall over the pit and has many of the warriors on display in a separate museum. Would you like to visit the site? Why do you think scientists worry about millions of tourists ascending upon a historical site? What are some important rules to remember when you visit a landmark like this?

FS-23226 Social Studies Made Simple ■ © Frank Schaffer Publications, Inc.

Inventions

Some of the world's greatest inventions came from China. Emperors encouraged the development of science. Paper and printing, gunpowder, the magnetic compass, porcelain, fireworks, kites, umbrellas, paper money, and iron casting are some Chinese inventions. Around the time of the Han dynasty the wheelbarrow, the saddle, a type of seismograph, the chain pump, hot-air balloons, the suspension bridge, paper, and the stern-post rudder were invented. Kites were invented to frighten the enemy in battle. Later they were flown to celebrate festivals. In the space below, design a kite of a dragon, phoenix, lion, or other animal. Your design should look like a Chinese kite with interesting shapes and parts.

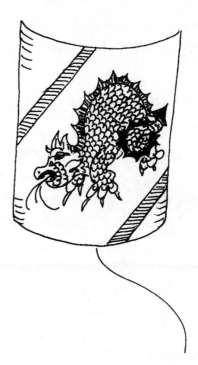

Try This!

Besides paper, which of the inventions mentioned above do you think was the most important? Explain why you think so. Then tell what you think the world would be like without the invention.

Ancient Crete

Time: 3000–1400 BC

Location: the island of Crete and other islands in the Aegean Sea

Significance: Europe's first civilization; the first great civilization of the Aegean world; a brilliant, rich civilization with skilled craftworkers, master builders, extensive trading, and a system of writing.

THE MYTH OF KING MINOS ·········· Class Activity ·····

In Greek mythology, Minos was the ruler of Crete. Minos used his powerful navy to rule over an extensive Aegean empire and required tribute from the conquered lands. Knossos was his palace, and a deadly Minotaur, a half-bull, half-man monster, lurked in a labyrinth beneath the palace. Theseus volunteered to be one of the 14 youths sent as tribute to be sacrificed to the Minotaur. Ariadne, daughter of the king, fell in love with Theseus, and she devised a plan. She gave Theseus a ball of thread which he fixed to the labyrinth's entrance. After killing the Minotaur, Theseus guided himself to safety by following the thread back to the entrance. Read aloud (or have your students read independently) the complete version of this myth. Discuss the characteristics of myths. What could be true about this myth? Why is it a Greek myth? Assign students the task of creating their own mythical monster and writing a myth about it. Include some action involving a maze. Illustrate the myth and make an overhead view of the maze.

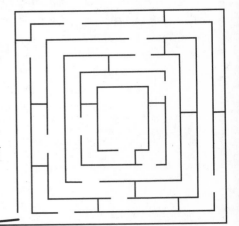

TRADE ·········· Class Activity ·····

The Minoan civilization was wealthy as a result of its trade with Greece, islands in the Aegean, Egypt, Syria, the Cyclades, Libya, Palestine, and Asia Minor. Minoan cargoes of timber, olive oil, wine, glazed pottery, stone jars, clay lamps, woolen cloth, bronze daggers, and silver items from Crete were exchanged for copper from Greece, obsidian from the Aegean isles, and tin and lapis lazuli from central Asia. Ask students to name the kinds of people who would be employed in such a far-reaching trading civilization. Consider governors; supervisors of irrigation projects, vineyards, and olive orchards; merchants and sea captains; priests and priestesses; artisans; artists; clerks; farmers and herders; laborers and serfs. Have students make a map that highlights Crete and its trading partners.

POTTERY

The Cretans made beautiful pottery. The shapes are elegant and the painted designs are complex. Many of the scenes are taken from plant and marine life. Others embody geometrical patterns—rosettes, discs, whorls, and comma-shaped signs. Among the finest examples are the Kamares-style vases with their polychrome designs on a black background. Kamares ware was crafted in delicate shapes copied from gold and silver vases and adorned with abstract designs in red and white on a lustrous background. Supply students with a large piece of construction paper. Have them draw an outline of a Kamares-style vase. Tell them to decorate the vase with authentic designs that make it worthy of being placed in a museum.

Art Project

Fresco Painting

Minoans had exquisite frescoes and painted reliefs on their houses and palaces. A fresco is a picture painted on the plaster of a wall while the plaster is still damp. This meant the artist had to be quick. Human figures are shown in profile, and artists always painted men red and the women white. The paintings show creativity in the choice of colors. Vegetation was painted in a variety of colors, but rarely in green. In one fresco, a blue ape is shown among the beasts. The works of art were usually religious, incorporating figures of men and women with animals and birds in flower-decked landscapes. Bull-leaping sports were a frequent theme in the frescoes at Knossos. The Minoans also loved the sea which gave them food, protection, and a means to trade. Lively fish and other sea creatures are painted on their walls and pottery. Students can make individual frescoes. First they should plan a Minoan design with a theme of the sea. Pour plaster of Paris into a container such as the lid of a shoebox. While the plaster is still damp, paint the picture on it with watercolors or tempera paint. Compare fresco painting with painting on canvas.

RELIGION

The double-headed ax was an important religious symbol of the Minoan civilization. It appears as a decoration in frescoes and on various objects. Actual axes have also been found in pottery and in gold. Another symbol of Minoan religion is the bull. Stylized horns, carved from massive blocks of stone, consecrated the rooms and hallways where they stood. Palace officials poured libations from vessels fashioned into the shape of a bull's head. On ceremonial occasions, the king may have worn a bull mask and, in this manner, created the legend of the Minotaur. A bull was also sacrificed to the mother goddess with a double-headed ax. Have students imagine that they can travel back in time and witness a Minoan religious ceremony. Then have each student write a short story that speculates about the origins of the double ax and bull as religious symbols.

Name _____

The Palace at Knossos

Much of our knowledge of Crete comes from archaeological work done on the palace of Knossos—the home of the powerful King Minos. In the palace, winding corridors jutting off in all directions connected a maze of more than a thousand rooms. Many of the interior walls consisted of multiple doors that could be opened to change the shape of a room. The rooms surrounded an open courtyard. To Greeks and other foreigners who were unfamiliar with its layout, the palace must have seemed a bewildering jumble, or a labyrinth.

The palace's wonderfully preserved wall paintings show how the people lived, the clothes they wore, and the entertainment they enjoyed. A complex system of pipes channeled the rainwater down through the building to deep underground drains, and fresh water traveled to the palace through a 10-mile network of terra-cotta pipes. Storerooms on the ground floor of the palace held hundreds of huge clay jars, called *pithoi.* The jars stored grain, olive oil, wine, and other trade goods. The total capacity of the pithoi exceeded 60,000 gallons.

Mycenaeans from the less sophisticated Greek mainland were awed by Knossos's size, intricacy, and rituals. From their visits, the legend of the great labyrinth, in which the Minotaur dwelled, developed. The Mycenaean word *labyrs* referred to the sacred double ax. The name *labyrinth* was probably used to identify the Knossos palace as the "house of the double ax."

Complete the following activities.

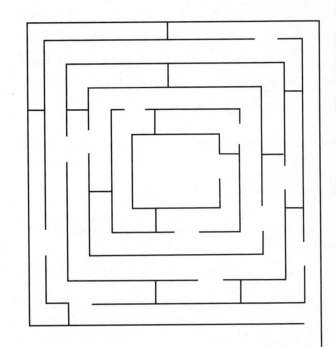

1. Imagine that you are principal for a day. You decide that learning would be more interesting if you turned the school into a labyrinth. Draw your plans for this unusual school and label the various rooms and corridors. In a short paragraph, write what you will be saying to the school board in defense of your plans.

2. Create an amazing maze that will confuse all of your friends. Using the myth of the Minotaur as an example, write a myth about your maze.

FS-23226 Social Studies Made Simple ▪ © Frank Schaffer Publications, Inc.

Ancient Greece

Time: 750 BC–323 BC

Location: mainland Greece, the islands in the Aegean Sea

Significance: world's first democracy, first people to examine the past critically and write down their findings, major advances in philosophy, science and medicine; known for literary, architectural and sculptural sophistication

IMAGINATIVE HISTORY
Class Activity

Greece

Wandering minstrels entertained Mycenaean nobles. The tales often told of the heroic deeds of the nobelmen's ancestors. These songs and ballads traveled along with colonists as they settled in Ionia. Mycenaean ruins lay everywhere; they looked like the work of great heroes, gods, or even giants. A ninth century poet, Homer, was the first and most famous epic poet to record some of these imaginative histories. *The Iliad,* one of two epic poems, tells the story of King Agamemnon of Mycenae and other Greek heroes who waged war against the city of Troy when Trojans kidnapped the Greek queen Helen. *The Odyssey,* the other epic poem, tells the adventures of the Greek hero, Odysseus, on his journey home from the war. The poems reminded Greeks of their forgotten heroes and led them to admire the accomplishments of their ancestors. After they have heard or read the story of the Trojan Horse, tell students to pretend to be one of the Greek soldiers inside the horse. Have them write a story about the soldier's opinion of the ploy, what it was like to be inside the horse, and what happened when the hoax was discovered.

GEOGRAPHY OF GREECE
Class Activity

Greece is mountainous with a complex coastline and numerous islands scattered throughout the Aegean and Adriatic seas. Inland, mountain ridges separate small, isolated, fertile plains. The sea, however, influenced Greek culture because it linked the communities for communication and trade. Supply children with an outline map of Greece. Students can use atlases and other reference materials to identify: Sparta, Mycenae, Corinth, Delphi, Athens, Rhodes, Crete, Peloponnese, Macedonia, Ithaca, Troy, Marathon, Thebes, Mount Olympus, the Aegean Sea, the Sea of Crete, the Ionian Sea, the Saronic Gulf, the Gulf of Corinth, and the Mediterranean Sea. Challenge students to name as many Greek islands as they can. Then give them 10 minutes to complete a list of the islands using reference materials. Have students collect brochures on the Greek islands from travel agents. Have them choose where they would go if they were given a dream vacation and have them write a story about their imagined experiences.

HISTORICAL DATES
····· **Class Activity** ·····

Use the table below to help students understand the order in which certain important battles took place. Students can decide which military battles they would consider important enough for a "top five" list. As students learn about other political, architectural, historical, and cultural events, they can add them to the table.

490 BC	The Greeks defeated the first Persian invasion at the Battle of Marathon.
480 BC	The Athenians defeated the Persian fleet at Salamis.
461–431 BC	The Golden Age of Athens
431–404 BC	Sparta defeated Athens in the Peloponnesian War.
371 BC	Thebes defeated Sparta.
338 BC	Philip II of Macedonia defeated the Greeks; Greece made part of Macedonia.
334–328 BC	Alexander the Great conquered the Persian Empire.
323 BC	Alexander the Great died, and the Hellenistic Age began.
197 BC	The Romans conquered Macedonia and Greece.
146 BC	Greece became a Roman province.

ANCIENT GREEK CATEGORIES
····· **Class Activity** ·····

By 600s BC, early Greek trading posts reached as far as Egypt. Other settlements reached southern Italy, Sicily, the western Mediterranean, and the eastern Black Sea. Greeks colonized the city-states of Paestum, Kroton, Syracuse, Carthage, Sparta, Argos, Mycenae, Corinth, Athens, Melos, Thera, Paros, Knossos, Lindos, Byzantion, and Salamis. Have students locate these places on an outline map. Discuss with your class the effects that the complex coastline of Greece would have on a unified country. Play "Ancient Greek Categories." Across the top of a piece of paper, have students write these column headings: Islands, Trading Posts and City-States, Mythological Hero or God, and Famous Person. Randomly choose a letter of the alphabet. Tell students they have three minutes to think of an answer for each category that begins with that letter. One point can be awarded for each correct answer. Award two points if a student has an answer that no one else in the class thought of.

THE GOLDEN AGE OF ATHENS
····· **Class Activity** ·····

During the Golden Age of Greece (500–350 BC), life for most people was good. Crafts, trade, and agriculture flourished. The new wealth made it possible for education, literature, architecture, mathematics, science, and philosophy to develop more fully. Ask students which period of history in the United States they would label as the Golden Age. After students study ancient Greece, have them list the people and events that led to historians calling the period "golden."

FS-23226 *Social Studies Made Simple* ▪ © Frank Schaffer Publications, Inc.

STONE MASTERPIECES · Class Activity ····

The Greek sculptors were able to turn hard stone into pieces of art. Sculptures of men, women, children, gods, and athletes decorated buildings and commemorated gods and famous people. The most famous Greek sculptor was Phidias. He carved the famous statue of Zeus at Olympia and many others located around the Parthenon, including the large statue of Athena. Many statues were made as offerings to gods or goddesses. Have students research a famous piece of Greek sculpture, make a drawing of it, and critique it from the viewpoint of an artist. Then have them add a few sentences about the importance of the sculpture from the viewpoint of an archaeologist.

THE GREEK ALPHABET · Class Activity ····

alpha	beta	gamma	delta	epsilon
A α	B β	Γ γ	Δ δ	E ε
zeta	**eta**	**theta**	**iota**	**kappa**
Z ζ	H η	Θ q	I ι	K κ
lambda	**mu**	**nu**	**xi**	**omicron**
Λ λ	M μ	N ν	X x	O o
pi	**rho**	**sigma**	**tau**	**upsilon**
Π π	P ρ	Σ σ,V	T τ	Υ υ
phi	**chi**	**psi**	**omega**	
F φ	X χ	Ψ ψ	Ω ω	

The very early Greeks traveled to Phoenicia and brought back knowledge of the Phoenician alphabet that later became the basis for the Greek alphabet. In lands such as Egypt and China, whose scripts consisted of hundreds of symbols, reading and writing was left to scribes and scholars. Learning Greek was much easier, and most Greek males and many Greek females learned to read. Point out that the Greek alphabet has fewer letters than the English alphabet. Challenge students to write messages to friends using the Greek alphabet as a code. Point out that many Greek words from the sciences, arts, and politics are similar to English words. Ask student to identify the English word that corresponds to *astronomia*, *aster*, *galaxia*, *kometes*, *meloida*, *choros*, *komoidia*, *historia*, *metropolis*, *demokratia*, and *schole*. Challenge students to find other words with Greek roots.

THE OLYMPIC GAMES

Group Activity

The first Olympic Games were held in 776 BC and then every four years until AD 394. The games originated with a religious festival held at Olympia, a sanctuary to the god Zeus. Athletes came from all over Greece, even during times of war. In 420 BC, during the Peloponnesian War, Sparta was banned from the Olympic games for hostile acts, but the contests went forward—under armed guard. Women could not take part in, or even watch, the games. An exception was made for the priestesses of the temple at Olympia. Athletes participated in the pancratium contest, a combination of wrestling and boxing; chariot races; horseback racing; and a foot race in full armor, as well as traditional track and field events. Have students compare the modern Olympic Games with the ancient games. What are the sports that are official now which were not part of the early Greek games? Have students imagine that they can travel forward in time to plan for the Olympics of 2040. They will work in one of the Olympic Committees that decide on two new events which will be allowed in 2040, plan the official opening ceremony, design the outfit for the team from the United States for the opening ceremony, or design a new gold medal for the games.

THE BEST OF SCIENCE

Class Activity

Greek scientists were also philosophers. Pythagoras taught and wrote about mathematics, astronomy, music, and religion. He thought that purity of bodies and minds could be gained through science and mathematics. His theories influenced Plato and Aristotle. He is best known for the Pythagorean Theorem—in a right triangle the square of the hypotenuse equals the sum of the squares of the other two sides. Create a book, *Greek Scientists and Mathematicians*. Each student or small group of students can make a page for the book for each scientist or mathematician. Include a short biography, famous works or ideas, a "best known for" page, and a picture, diagram, or drawing that clarifies the information. Some of the best known scientists include

Archimedes (principle of the lever),	*Erastosthenes* (earth's circumference),
Theophrastus (first scientific botanist),	*Pythagoras* (mathematics),
Heraclitus (theory on atoms),	*Asclepiades* (doctor),
Aristarchus (astronomer),	*Hippocrates* (founder of modern medicine),
Ptolemy I (founded a research center),	*Euclid* (geometry),
Hipparchus (inventor of trigonometry),	*Appollonius* (discoverer of conic sections),
Herodotus ("father of history"),	*Thucydides* (historian),
Herophilus (experimental anatomy),	*Anaxagoras* (discovered that the moon reflected sunlight).

FS-23226 Social Studies Made Simple ■ © Frank Schaffer Publications, Inc.

WOMEN'S RIGHTS

Class Activity

The women of Crete and Mycenaea had more rights than the women who lived in Athens during the Golden Age. In Athens, women were forbidden to vote, attend school, own property, work in businesses, or attend athletic events. Women's main roles were to manage the household and raise the children. Girls did not attend school, but some wealthy families hired private tutors who taught their daughters to read and write. By the end of the Golden Age, women were gaining more freedoms. Plato welcomed both men and women to his academy, and Hippocrates trained many women to become doctors. By the time of Alexander the Great, women were allowed to freely walk in the streets and

participate in philosophy, the sciences, and the arts. Tell students to imagine that they have been invited to travel back in time for a oratory contest. They will be allowed to present a one-minute speech to the members of general assembly in support of allowing women to attend public functions. The assembly may vote to change the laws if the members think the speeches are convincing. Speeches can be given either to the class or a small group.

DEMOCRACY

Class Activity

Over the course of a thousand years, ancient Greece slowly moved from rule by kings to rule by the people. In Athens, every free man over the age of 21 born to Athenian parents was automatically a member of the city's main governing body, the Assembly. Every nine days the Assembly met to decide on laws and policies. Every citizen had a vote and the right to present his opinions before the Assembly. A lottery system gave every citizen an equal chance to work in nearly every part

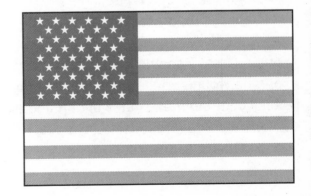

of government. The Greek system has been called the broadest and the most equal democracy in history. But the democracy did not include everyone. A large group of foreigners, called metics; slaves, most of whom were captured in wars; and women were excluded from political power. Have students debate which style of tales democracy provides more equality—the Greek or the American.

Spotlight on Athens

Athens, a port city on the Aegean, was one of the world's first democracies. A trade center, it welcomed immigrants and encouraged new ideas and public debate. Athens became the most powerful of the Greek city-states. At first, kings ruled; then elected officials called *archons* headed the government. When civil war between the very rich and the poor of Athens threatened, Solon (594 BC), an *archon*, made several important reforms, but they failed to solve the problem. In 561 BC, Pisistratus, an army commander, seized power. Pisistratus reduced the power of the wealthy and made improvements in the city. About 508 BC, the Athenians adopted a new constitution proposed by Cleisthenes. Under Cleisthenes's system, all men registered as citizens when they reached age 18. A 500-member council was chosen each year by drawing lots. The council prepared business for the general assembly. Unpopular politicians could be banished for 10 years if more than 6,000 votes were cast against them.

The **acropolis** was the center of the city-state. It started out as a fortified citadel built on top of a hill. Temples, simple at first, but later much more elaborate, were added. In 480 BC, the Persian army captured Athens and destroyed most of the buildings on the acropolis. In 447 BC, Athenians led by Pericles started rebuilding the acropolis. Ictinus and Mnesicles, architects and builders, and Phidias, a famous sculptor, assisted. Dominating the acropolis was the Parthenon, the marble temple of the goddess Athena. Inside the temple stood a huge gold and ivory statue of Athena. The Propylaea, the huge monumental entrance, guarded the only way to enter to the acropolis. Two other important temples were the Erechtheion, with marble statues of women instead of columns, and the temple of Athena Nike. Below the acropolis were beautiful public squares, the homes of the people, and the *agora*, the marketplace or open meeting space.

A special road—the Panathenaic Way—led up from the *agora* to the acropolis. Every four years during the celebration of the Great Panathenaea, held in honor of Athena, a huge parade wound up the Panathenaic Way. This procession is the main subject of the frieze that went around all four sides of the Parthenon. After Alexander the Great unified Greece, the city of Athens added gymnasia, schools, libraries, public baths, and lavatories.

(continued on page 62)

FS-23226 *Social Studies Made Simple* • © Frank Schaffer Publications, Inc.

Spotlight on Athens *(continued)*

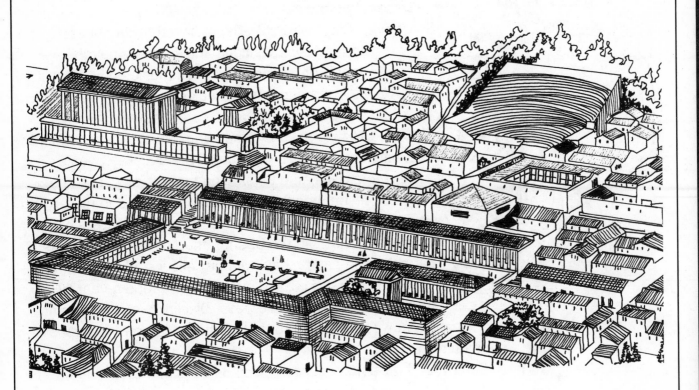

Try This!

1. Many of the sculptures from the Parthenon were brought to England by Lord Elgin, the British ambassador to the Ottoman court. The Elgin Marbles can be seen today in the British Museum. In a letter to the British Museum, explain why you think the Elgin Marbles should be returned to Greece. Then write the response from the viewpoint of the museum director.

2. Make a "Guide to Ancient Athens" in the form of a travel brochure. Include architectural wonders, fascinating facts of history, and sites to interest travelers. Add drawings, maps, and information about the climate and what to wear.

Sparta

Sparta, founded by the Dorians, was located 150 miles from Athens and far from the sea. It was located at the foot of Mount Taygettus in the valley of the Eurotas River where high mountains formed natural defenses.

Spartans disapproved of trade, of contact with outsiders, and of new inventions and ideas. Although Sparta produced fine crafts, music and poetry, it was one of the few Greek city-states that never developed a democracy. Throughout its history, Sparta was ruled by kings and nobles. Disagreement with its rulers was punished by death. The people's lives were dedicated to learning the arts of war. At the age of seven, healthy boys were introduced to military training and were required to undergo yearly tests of fitness and discipline. A Spartan man had to sleep in the barracks and have meals with his fellow soldiers until he was 30 years old. Each male had to spend a year living on his own in the wilderness. Discipline started at birth, for any baby that was weak or in poor health was left on the slopes of the mountain to die.

Each year the Spartan citizens elected five governors, called *ephoroi*, from amongst themselves. They were responsible for the discipline of the state and acted as presidents at state meetings. Justice was administered by a council of 29 men who were all over 60 years of age. Non-citizens in Sparta were either *periokoi* or *helots*. The periokoi were free men who were allowed to trade and serve in the army even though they did not have the rights of citizens. Helots were the descendants of the original inhabitants of the area. They farmed the land and did the heavy work for Spartan overlords. The Spartans are not famous for their glorious temples or lasting works of art or literature. But their army was the strongest and bravest in all the ancient world.

Complete the following activity.

Make two columns on a piece of paper. Label one "Pro" and the other "Con." Then under the appropriate column, list the pros and cons of living in Sparta. Do the same thing for the city of Athens. Explain in which city you would have liked to live as a teenager and give the reasons for your decision.

Greek Architecture

Greek temples were homes for gods so Greek architecture designed them to be beautiful as a tribute to the gods. The temples were designed simply, with a pillared porch on all sides of a rectangular structure. Columns, made in cylindrical sections and held together with metal pegs, bore the weight of the roof. The columns were lifted into position with ropes and pulleys. Temples were made of limestone or marble, with roofs and ceilings of wood.

The Greek architects used Doric, Ionic, and Corinthian columns in their buildings. **Doric** columns are thick and powerful. They have no base but are topped with a plain, round capital. Most Athenian temples, including the famous Parthenon in Athens, were built in the strong, simple Doric style used in mainland Greece and the colonies in southern Italy and Sicily. **Ionic** columns are taller and more slender than Doric, with a rounded base and a scroll-shaped capital. They usually had 24 flutes—more than a Doric column. The Temple of Athena Nike at the gateway of the acropolis is one of the oldest surviving Ionic buildings in Athens. **Corinthian** is the most elaborate style. It was first used in the city-state of Corinth. The Corinthian order adopted the Ionic columns but added capitals intricately carved with delicate acanthus leaf patterns. This ornate style was rarely used in the temples of Greece's Golden Age but often appeared in later Roman temples.

Identify each architectural order.

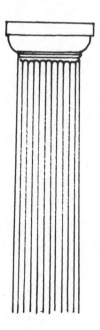
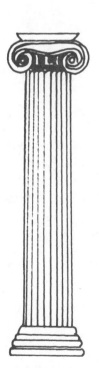
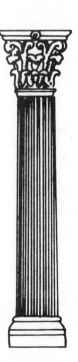

_____   _____   _____

(continued on page 65)

Greek Architecture (continued)

Friezes were common as temple decorations. Usually a master sculptor designed the frieze and skilled craftsmen did the actual carving. Two of the most famous Greek friezes appear on the temple of Zeus at Olympia and the Parthenon in Athens, designed by Phidias. Friezes commonly show the figures of gods or heroes. The Olympia frieze shows the twelve labors of Hercules. The frieze in the Parthenon depicts a religious festival in honor of Athena. The marble frieze, high on the outside of the main building near the ceiling or colonnade, appeared on all four sides of the building. Today the friezes are in original marble or stone, but Greeks painted them in red and blue, with gold and green accents.

1. Use these architectural terms to label the parts of this simplified Greek temple. You may use a dictionary if necessary.

peristyle,

capital,

shaft,

base,

entablature,

frieze,

cornice,

pediment

2. Explain what you like about each of the three orders of Greek architecture.

Doric: _____

Ionic: _____

Corinthian: _____

Try This! Modern courthouses, parliament buildings, museums, art galleries, war memorials, and churches sometimes copy Greek architecture. Are there any examples in your town or city? If not, look at pictures of the public buildings in Washington, D.C. Name the building and tell what order of architecture is used.

FS-23226 Social Studies Made Simple • © Frank Schaffer Publications, Inc.

Greek Gods and Mythology

The Greeks believed in many gods. Each town, stream, grove of trees, and act of nature had its special god. Because there were so many gods, the acropolis in most towns became a holy place with many temples.

The most important gods of the classical era were called the Olympians because their home was Mount Olympus. The Greeks believed that Zeus sat on a golden throne atop Mount Olympus and ruled all other gods. No matter where they lived, Greeks worshipped Zeus and his family of gods. They also worshipped thousands of minor gods and spirits.

Find out more about the Greek gods by doing research about them. Then complete the following activities:

1. The twelve Olympian gods are listed below. Write on the line the area or areas of concern of each god or goddess.

Zeus _____ Hera _____

Hestia _____ Demeter _____

Poseidon _____ Athena _____

Aphrodite _____ Hephaestus _____

Ares _____ Hermes _____

Apollo _____ Artemis _____

2. Explain the role of these lesser gods or spirits:

    The Fates   The Graces   The Harpies

    The Hours   The Muses   The Centaurs

3. The Greeks had a god or spirit for every object or force of nature—but they did not know about modern technology. With the power of Zeus, create a god or goddess for the telephone, the computer, or the automobile. Explain your choice.

Name _____

The Greek Theater

The ancient Greeks staged the first tragedies for which we have a written record in 534 BC at the Festival of Dionysus in Athens. Although other cultures had undoubtedly acted out stories in one form or another, Greeks were the first to stage drama in a formal way.

Tradition says that Thespis of Icaria was the first to use an actor as part of his poetry choruses. The audience was fascinated because the actor was masked, was not singing his own verses, and was impersonating another person. Soon, other poets like Aeschylus and Sophocles added actors. The innovation was very popular and made theater-going one of the most popular pastimes in ancient Greece. In Athens, thousands of people attended the drama festivals.

Greek theaters were spectacular outdoor structures. The theater at Epidaurus seated 14,000 people. The auditorium consisted of a curved viewing section in a semicircular bowl cut into the surface of the hillside. Its shape amplified the sound and ensured that everyone in the audience had a clear view of the action. All of the actors were men—even for the female parts— and they played their roles on a flat, circular area called the orchestra. Each actor played several parts, but since the characters wore masks, it was possible to change quickly from role to role. The masks also indicated emotions such as sadness, anger, or mirth.

The chorus was essential to Greek drama. The chorus made sure that the audience understood the important ideas in the drama by commenting on the play's action and addressing the audience directly. Since these early plays were religious, it was very important that the audience understood the religious "truth" that was central to the drama. In early plays, the chorus sang their parts; later they also danced. As the drama became more popular, plays about legendary Greek heroes were added. By the fifth century BC, both tragedies and comedies were performed. Many of these plays have survived to the present time. Plays were put on about once a month and the performance lasted all day.

1. Imagine that you can travel back in time to attend a Greek play. Write a letter home telling about the auditorium, the behavior of the audience, the play you saw, the costumes, chorus, and masks, and the amplifying system.

2. Make Greek drama masks showing the emotions of horror, joy, and anger.

Ancient Rome

Time: 753 BC–AD 476

Location: spread from Italy to Britain, the Persian Gulf, to Africa and Germany

Significance: once the mightiest empire on earth

THE INFLUENCE OF THE ETRUSCANS

Class Activity

Etruscans from central and northern Italy had been influenced by the Greeks and the city-state of Carthage. Latins, from the region south of Rome, interacted with the Etruscans to make up the Roman population. The Etruscans probably gave the city its name, introduced the Romans to the Greek alphabet, and gave Rome its religion. Etruscan potters and metalworkers were among the most advanced in Europe, and their skills also enriched Rome. Etruscan engineers taught the Romans to build bridges, roads, and arches, and Etruscan social customs, dress, lavish parties, chariot races, and hand-to-hand battle between slaves also became a part of the Roman society. In spite of this enormous influence, however, the Romans developed their own identity. They kept their Latin language and most of their own political and social institutions. Have students "delve into the past" to find out more about the Etruscans. Each student can focus on one particular area of interest. Have them demonstrate what they learned by making a collage, giving an oral report with visuals, or creating a skit.

THE REPUBLIC OF ROME

Group Activity

Bust of Julius Caesar

Rome was ruled by a series of Etruscan kings, but in 509 BC, the Roman people threw out the Etruscan king and vowed never to bow to any king in the future. They decided on a new form of government called a republic, a government run by elected representatives. Have students compare and contrast the governmental systems of republics and democracies. Discuss the origin of the word "republic" (from two Latin words, *res publica*, or "the affairs of the people"). The two main groups of officials in the Republic of Rome were the patricians, or nobles, and the plebeians, or commoners. Patricians were wealthy and came from the old aristocratic families. Most plebeians were farmers, tradesmen, artisans, or laborers. Only a relatively small portion of the population could take part in the government. At first only the patricians controlled the government and neither women nor slaves qualified as citizens. Do your students think that the Roman Republic represented the "the affairs of people?" Have them explain their viewpoints in small discussion groups. What is the consensus of the entire class? How is the word "plebeian" (or pleb) used in the English language?

THE *REPUBLIC TRIBUNE* NEWSPAPER

Class Activity

As the Roman republic grew, so did its system of public officials. By the time the Roman republic dissolved, the government included consuls, pro-consuls, praetors, and tribunes, quaestors, pontifexs, and censors for every aspect of Roman life. After students learn the jobs of each of the public officials, they can put together a newspaper called the *Republic Tribune,* or choose a title of their choice. Students should write the news of the Roman Republic and locate or draw appropriate visuals. Students can take the position of one of the officials and write an article from that official's perspective. For example, Increasamus Taxcerius, a quaestor, could write a story about tax collecting; and Casius Justicus, a praetor, might write a story about a bribery scandal. Other stories could be on the games, chariot races, battles, triumphal marches, a new temple or monument being built, or engineers who build the roads and aqueducts. Include an advice column, letters to the editor, and an editorial.

PAX ROMANA

Class Activity

Unlike many other dictators in history, the Roman Emperor Augustus ruled fairly from 44 BC to 14 AD. His peaceful and prosperous reign was called the Augustan Age and was the beginning of a long era of prosperity known as the *Pax Romana* or "great Roman peace." Most people looked back on the republican years as a time of trouble and chaos and were thankful for the order and good times Augustus had brought. He increased pay to the military and recruited 1,500 police for the city of Rome, which had a population exceeding one million. The police reduced the crime rate and the number of public riots. Augustus awarded provincial governors who did well and demoted those who did not. He reformed the tax system, increased trade, and improved living standards. He constructed harbors, aqueducts, and public buildings including the forum of Caesar, the Theater of Marcellus, and the first large public bath. He was especially interested in the arts and supported many writers and poets, including Virgil, Horace, and Ovid. Augustus died August 19, AD 14. Many people thought that Augustus was a good dictator. Do your students think that a dictator can be good? Would they be able to live in a dictatorship? Organize a class debate on whether Rome would have been better off as republic or a dictatorship.

A DEAD LANGUAGE?

Class Activity

One of the most important things the Romans left the world was their language. Latin gradually developed into French, Spanish, Portuguese, Italian, and Romanian—often referred to as the Romance languages. Latin also influenced the Germanic tongues of the Angles and Saxons and eventually mixed with Latin and French to form the English language. More than half the words in English are of Latin origin. Give students 20 minutes to see how many English words with Latin roots they can find in a dictionary. Talk about Latin roots and how knowing a few roots will make learning vocabulary easier.

FS-23226 *Social Studies Made Simple* ■ © Frank Schaffer Publications, Inc.

ROMAN NUMERALS

Roman Numerals		
I = 1	VI = 6	L = 50
II = 2	VII = 7	C = 100
III = 3	VIII = 8	D = 500
IV = 4	IX = 9	M = 1000
V = 5	X = 10	

The Romans used a numbering system which became known as Roman numerals. The Romans had no sign for zero so arithmetic using Roman numerals is difficult. Work with your class to find other differences and similarities between the Roman system and the Arabic system of numbers. Ask your class if they know of places where they might see Roman numerals today. Explain the concepts behind writing the numerals and then have them practice writing numerals. Write three or four large numbers on the chalkboard which students can work on if they have a few free minutes. At the end of the school day, give the answers.

ROMAN BUILDING GENIUS—ROADS

The Romans built roads to serve the military needs of a far-reaching empire. On good roads, Roman troops could travel more than 30 miles in a day. Building a road was a complex engineering feat. The roadbed had to be higher in the center so that water would run off into ditches at the roadsides. The roads needed to provide a firm foundation for heavy loads, so the roads were built with compact layers of sand, small stones, gravel, and, finally, paving stones on top. The paving stones were polished and cut at an angle. Many Roman roads continued to be used throughout the Middle Ages; some are still in use today. Have teams of students do research to collect Roman road facts and then have a Roman Road Trivia game between two teams of students.

WOMEN AND SLAVES

In early Roman times, women had few rights, but during the last two centuries of the republic, women won the right to divorce their husbands and receive a better education. By about 50 AD, Roman women were nearly equal to men. They attended public baths, festivals, games, and could discuss and write about politics. Some women even competed in hunting, fencing, and wrestling. Discuss equal rights for women in sports. Can women compete in all sports? Should they be able to? Do students think that women in the last part of the twentieth century have equal rights with men?

ROMAN UNEMPLOYMENT

In the early empire, Roman slaves worked on farms or lived in cities in a relatively comfortable style. Slaves could own property and even hold slaves of their own. The Romans turned over so many of their chores and business tasks to slaves that hundreds of thousands of free Romans could not find work. The unemployment caused much idleness and dissatisfaction. Unemployed Romans needed government handouts so they would not starve. Ask your students what would have been their policy toward slavery if they had been emperor of Rome. What would have been the immediate problems if the slaves had been freed? What would have been the long-range results?

The Roman Forum

At the city center of Roman cities was the forum, an open courtyard where the townspeople gathered to discuss their town's affairs or to listen to speeches by government officials. The forum was also the marketplace for merchants and farmers. Most government buildings, eating houses, public toilets, and many temples were grouped around the forum. It was the commercial, religious, and political center of the city.

The tomb of Romulus was located in the forum. Every road that led to Rome was measured from the "golden milestone" in the forum. The most splendid collection of temples, public buildings and commemorative statues ever assembled in the ancient world bordered the Roman forum. The Via Sacra or Sacred Way, which ran along one side of the Forum and then climbed the Capitoline Hill, was the most famous street in ancient Rome. Victorious generals rode in triumphal processions along the Via Sacra as did religious procession and grand funerals.

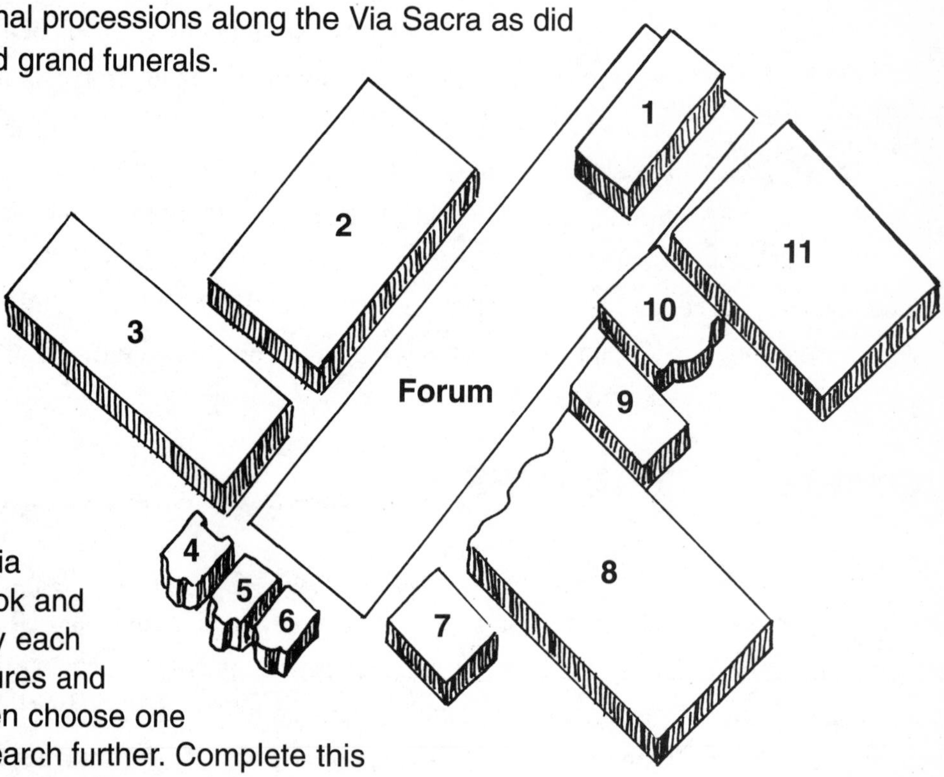

Forum

Take a tour along the Via Sacra. Use your textbook and other sources to identify each of the numbered structures and explain its function. Then choose one of the structures to research further. Complete this Roman Forum Fact Sheet for the structure that you chose.

Name of Structure: _____

Purpose of Structure: _____

When Built: _____

Historical Information: _____

Sketch of Structure: _____

Temples, Gods, and Goddesses

The Romans worshipped many gods, goddesses, demigods, and spirits. Each of the temples honored a different one. Usually, only special priests or priestesses and their assistants were allowed inside the temples. Worshippers gathered outside. The Pantheon, however, allowed worshippers inside. A large, round temple designed with interior beauty in mind, the Pantheon was built in 25 BC by Agrippa, Augustus' son-in-law. The rotunda was added by Hadrian. The Pantheon had eight recesses, with one forming the entrance and the other seven housing statues of the seven major Roman gods. A 30-foot wide *oculus,* or round opening, in the top of the dome illuminated the interior. The walls were 21-feet thick, built of concrete, and faced in marble. The Pantheon was converted into a church in the seventh century AD.

The Romans borrowed many of their gods and goddesses from the Greeks. Complete this chart with the name of the Roman god, the attributes of both the Greek and Roman gods, and their symbols.

Greek God	Roman God	Attributes	Symbols
Zeus			
Hera			
Athena			
Apollo			
Artemis			
Hermes			
Hephaestus			
Hestia			
Ares			
Aphrodite			
Demeter			
Poseidon			

Roman Building Genius

Romans were master builders using specially trained workers and lifting devices such as levers, winches, and tackle to move heavy material into place, but they borrowed their architecture from the Greeks. The Corinthian order was especially popular for its rich decoration. The composite style, a combination of Corinthian and Ionic styles, was also popular. Both styles adorned temples, government buildings, baths, amphitheaters, theaters, and circuses.

The Roman arch became a symbol of Roman might. Although the Greeks also used arches, the Romans introduced innovations. The Roman arch appeared in bridges, sewers, aqueducts, and triumphal gateways that honored victorious generals and emperors. An arch has several parts including the piers, wedge-shaped blocks, or *voussoirs,* and the keystone. The Romans created the tunnel or barrel vault which allowed them to build large buildings by modifying the arch. A series of arches lessened the stress on the piers and reduced the cost for projects such as the Roman aqueduct system, which brought water into towns all over the Roman empire. Because water cannot flow uphill, the engineers built huge bridges, called aqueducts, to carry the water pipes across valleys. Some aqueduct systems were two or three tiers high and carried water from its source to large cities thirty or more miles away. The Greek historian Strabo visited Rome in the first century AD, and observed that "such is the quantity of water brought in by the aqueducts, that veritable rivers flow through the city and its sewers: almost every house has cisterns, waterpipes, and copious fountains."

Roman builders used fired bricks and developed concrete by mixing a rich volcanic sand, *pozzolana,* with rubble. Concrete was used to make the huge vaulted halls of the imperial palaces, baths, and other buildings.

Identify and label the parts of the arch. Then label the arch, barrel vault, or tunnel.

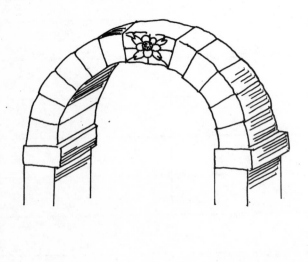
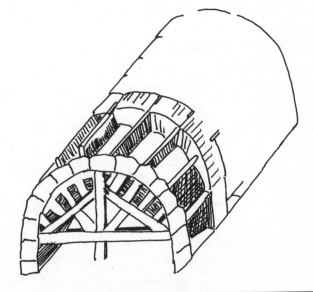

Roman Baths

Few Roman houses had their own baths, but the huge public baths more than made up for the lack. The largest Roman baths were built in 212 AD. They covered 25 acres. Workmen paved the floors with marble and mosaics and covered the walls with mosaics and gilded stucco work. Marble columns decorated vaulted rooms 98 feet high. Sixteen hundred bathers could use the baths at once.

Men used the baths to exercise, play games, meet friends, chat, relax, and get clean. Women also went to get clean, but they also enjoyed meeting friends, exercising in the gymnasium, and playing games. Larger baths even had a library, massage parlor, haircutting salon, and fast-food vendors.

Bathing was a ritual. After arriving, the bather undressed, rubbed oil into the skin, and proceeded to the exercise yard. Hot and sweaty from exercise, the bather proceeded to a very hot room, rather like a sauna. Then it was on to a large domed room where he or she sat in a pool of very hot water. Bathers scraped their skins to remove all impurities after the hot bath, progressed to a lukewarm pool, and finally into a cold pool.

Water for the hot pool was heated in huge tanks over a furnace. Hot air from the furnace flowed through a network of channels under the floor and through pipes in the walls to heat the rooms.

Complete the following activities:

1. Each of these terms is the name for a part of the Roman baths. Define each Latin word:

   A. thermae   **E.** caldarium

   B. laconicum   **F.** gymnasium

   C. frigidarium   **G.** tepidarium

   D. unctuarium

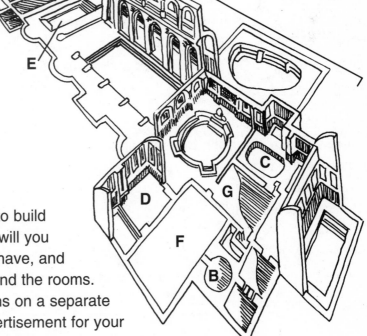

2. Imagine that you have been asked to build the biggest and best bath yet. How will you build the bath, what rooms will you have, and how will you decorate the building and the rooms. Make your drawings and descriptions on a separate piece of paper. Then create an advertisement for your spectacular thermae.

FS-23226 Social Studies Made Simple ■ © Frank Schaffer Publications, Inc.

SOCIAL STUDIES

• Ancient Rome •

Spotlight on Roman Entertainment

During Augustus' reign, 115 separate holidays drew people to feasts, races, contests, and dramas. The number rose to 200 holidays a year during some emperors' reigns! On these public holidays, Romans visited an amphitheater, theater, or circus.

The Theater of Pomepy seated 27,000 people. Elaborately costumed and masked actors tried to win the audience's praise with dancing, music, and mime and spectacular visual effects, like simulated battles and rainstorms. As with Greek theater, Roman shows started as religious festivals and evolved into original performances of mime and pantomime involving one actor dancing and miming a story from Greek legend.

The Coliseum in Rome held about 48,000 people and was so well-designed that everyone could get in and out of the building within a few minutes. The secret was in the skilled use of arched vaults and the corridors and stairways leading to the seating. The attractions at the Coliseum were also grimly efficient. Roman citizens gathered at the Coliseum to watch animals and other people being killed. Gladiators fought each other or wild animals. Often chosen from the ranks of slaves or criminals, gladiators attended special schools where they learned to fight. They wore masked helmets and armor and used a short sword called a *gladius.* Sometimes, gladiators fought North African animals such as tigers, elephants, leopards, panthers, and crocodiles. At other times, criminals or Christians were hunted by the animals. During the reign of Titus, 5,000 animals died in a single day. Emperor Trajan exceeded this number when more than 6,000 wild animals were killed.

At the Circus Maximus, Romans watched chariot races on a huge oval track. The races were very exciting, with frequent spills and crashes. Good charioteers were popular heroes. There were about 24 races a day and people enjoyed them sitting on cushions and eating snacks sold by vendors. The Circus Maximus had over 250,000 seats. Once, a collapse of the seating killed 13,000 people.

Try This!

Some Roman sports were extremely cruel. Write a letter to a Roman emperor pleading with him to change the entertainment in the Coliseum. Think about the ways that we might show cruelty in modern sports and make a list of them on the back of this page. Are there any similarities between the events that we see in coliseums and those the Romans saw in the Coliseum?

FS-23226 Social Studies Made Simple ▪ © Frank Schaffer Publications, Inc.

Answer Key

Page 3

1. Accept responses that show thought and understanding.
2. Students' stories may include descriptions of the hunters, the animals, the weapons, the countryside, and other details. Drawings should show some of the same elements.
3. Accept all reasonable attempts.
4. Accept all responses.

Page 5

Possible responses may include the role of vultures in preparing bodies for burial; the fact that the skull was separated from the body before burial; that bulls and leopards were strong and fierce animals which were often admired or even hunted.

Try This: Students' drawings, descriptions, and stories should be consistent with each other.

Page 6

1. If chemical analysis of the obsidian tools found at Çatal Hüyük showed that the obsidian came from Cyprus, and the areas now in modern Israel, Lebanon, and Syria, scientists may have concluded that trade routes existed among these locations and Çatal Hüyük.
2. Accept drawings and descriptions that show thought and understanding of Çatal Hüyük's culture.
3. Accept reasonable responses.

Try This: Accept reasonable lists.

Page 9

1. **a.** Farmers carried water to their fields.
   b. Farmers made narrow breaks in natural levees along the riverbanks and diverted water onto the fields.
   c. Farmers made small mud dams and collected water in basins.
   d. Farmers used shadufs to bring water from the dams to the fields.
   e. Groups of workers made long canals.
2. Students' stories should show awareness of the differences between Sumerian life and modern life.
3. The lists should show that students understand the problems of construction and maintenance of the cities and irrigation systems. The lists should also show a basic understanding of ways to organize people to accomplish the necessary tasks.

Page 10

1. Messages should correctly use the cuneiform chart.
2. Allow students to express creativity in this activity.
3. The symbols used in the signs should be understandable to people who speak other languages.

Page 11

Accept stories which reflect creativity and thought.

Page 14

1. Students' lists of situations and laws should be realistic.
2. Responses will vary.

Page 20

Designs created by the students should be appropriate in style and use materials available to ancient Egyptians. Statements should list the materials, where the materials came from, and the way in which the house meets the stated requirements.

Page 21

Students' selections and costumes will vary.

Page 22

1. Accept drawings that include Egyptian elements and styles.
2. Accept amulets which show attempts to include Egyptian elements.
3. The drawings of jewelry will vary.

Page 23

1. Possible responses include masks for hockey goalies, fencers, baseball catchers, Halloween costumes, Mardi Gras, blindman's bluff, hide-and-seek, and those used by painters or chemical workers.
2. **d.** good luck charm; **f.** rules for mummification; **b.** containers for organs; **a.** large outer coffin; **e.** salt; **c.** prevent a body from decaying
3. Drawings will vary. Religious influence on architecture may include church steeples, stained glass, minarets, Islamic geometric decorations, and so on.

Pages 24–25

1. Answers will vary.
2. Students' messages for Khafre will vary.

Page 26

From left to right: Horus, Osiris, Hathor, Isis, Bastet, Thoth, Anubis, Amon-re, Ptah

Page 29

1. Possible responses include that the cobra is dangerous and impressive; the cobra strikes silently and swiftly; it is not afraid of enemies.
2. Students' designs will vary.
3. The comparison drawings may show that the Kushite pyramids were smaller, steeper, the mummy was put under the pyramid, not in it, and that the mummy may be lying on a bed rather than in a sarcophagus.

Page 34

Christianity: Jesus; the *Bible* (Old and New Testament); practiced worldwide

Hinduism: many gods, especially Brahman; the Vedas and Upanishads; practiced in India and many other countries

Judaism: Abraham and other Old Testament figures; the Old Testament especially the Torah; practiced in Israel and many countries

Buddhism: Siddhartha Gautama, the Buddha; the teachings of Buddha; practiced mainly in Asian countries, but also worldwide

Page 35

Brahma, Vishnu, Krishna, Shiva

Page 36

1. Students' interview collections should reflect an accurate picture of life in ancient India.
2. Accept all myths which explain how elephants got their trunks.
3. Accept all appropriate stories.

Page 41

1. The plagues included water turning to blood, frogs swarming over the land, gnats, flies, pestilence and death of livestock, boils, hail, locusts, darkness, and death of the first-born child.
2. Accept all proposed legends.
3. Accept all stories that deal with the story elements.

Page 42

1. Possible responses: because they are very old, they may be more accurate than later transcriptions; some of them may contain unknown historical material; some of them may contain unknown religious material
2. **a.** There is a break in the earth's crust.
   b. the River Jordan

Page 49

Students' posters will vary.
Students' essays will vary.

Page 50

1. **conscript:** a person forced into service as a worker
   dynasty: a succession of rulers from the same family or line
   nomads: people who have no fixed home
2. Accept students' legends.

Page 51

1. Accept diary entries that reflect understanding of an archaeologist's possible reactions to the discovery of the terra-cotta soldiers.
2. Possible responses may cite factors such as vandalism, pollution, erosion, or funguses such as those at the Lascaux Cave. Rules to remember should consider safety, consideration, and preservation of the site.

Page 52

Drawings will vary.
Try This: Students' responses will vary.

Page 55

1. Students' plans and paragraphs will vary.
2. Students' mazes should be functional.

Pages 61–62

Try This: 1. Students' writings about the Elgin Marbles should show understanding of the issues. **2.** Students' brochures should show the results of their research about Athens.

Page 63

Possible "Pro" responses for Sparta include a strong army, more responsibility for women, discipline and training.

Possible "Con" responses for Sparta include emphasis on war and power, treatment of babies who were not "fit," and enslavement of the helots.

Possible "Pro" responses for Athens include the development of democracy, art, theater, poetry, architecture, education, and philosophy.

Possible "Con" responses for Athens include slavery and the treatment of women.

Page 64

From left to right: Doric, Ionic, Corinthian

Page 65

1.

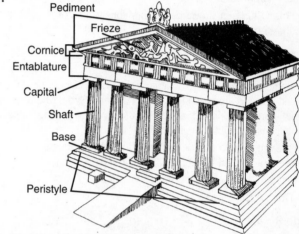

2. Accept responses which reflect thought and consideration of the three orders of Greek architecture.

Try This: Answers will vary.

Page 66

1. **Zeus** ruler of the other gods and goddesses
   Hera wife of Zeus, protector of marriage and women
   Hestia goddess of the hearth
   Demeter goddess of agriculture
   Poseidon god of earthquakes and the ocean
   Athena goddess of wisdom and war
   Aphrodite goddess of love
   Hephaestus blacksmith of the gods
   Ares god of war
   Hermes messenger of the gods
   Apollo god of music, light, medicine, and poetry
   Artemis goddess of hunting and childbirth
2. **the Fates** three goddesses who controlled the destiny of every person
   the Graces three daughters of Zeus, were goddesses of the arts
   the Harpies mythical beings who were half-woman, half-bird
   the Hours goddesses of the changing seasons
   the Muses nine goddess of various arts and sciences
   the Centaurs mythical beings who were half-man, half-horse
3. Answers will vary but should show originality.

FS-23226 Social Studies Made Simple ■ © Frank Schaffer Publications, Inc.